People & Boats

A History of the Louth Canal

by

Stuart M. Sizer & Josephine Clark

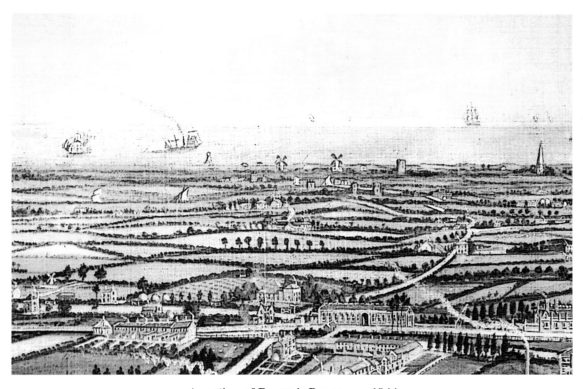

A section of Brown's Panorama 1844
where he showed Louth Navigation crossing the marsh towards Tetney Lock

Edited by John Stanbridge

ISBN
ISB10 0-953 645 1-1-8
ISB13 978-0-953 645 1-1-4

A view of the Navigation Warehouse & the canal basin from Riverhead Road, c.1900

Published by

Louth Navigation Trust
Registered Charity No 1057398

Navigation Warehouse, Riverhead Road, Louth, Lincolnshire LN11 0DA

As part of the Louth Navigation Trust History Project: www.louthcanal.org.uk
Any profits from the book will be used towards the objects of the History Project

The illustrations are from the collection of S. M. Sizer or the archives of the Louth
Navigation Trust except for the sections from Brown's Panorama 1844, courtesy of
Louth Town Council

Printed by Allinson Print & Supplies,
Allinson House, Lincoln Way, Fairfield Industrial Estate, Louth, Lincs. LN11 0LS.
Telephone: 01507 606661. Fax. 01507 600434.

Hidden away to the east of the town of Louth is what remains of a once important and profitable part of Louth's past, The Louth Navigation. 'I didn't know all this was here', or 'There's so much of interest to be seen', is the common remark from people I take round what is left of the Riverhead area of the Louth Canal.

Louth was once a bustling inland port with ships arriving from the Yorkshire region as well as those from far away ports such as London. They brought all manner of goods and wares with them, returning with corn and wool along with other exports.

Why did we need a Canal in the first place? How did it grow and why did it cease to exist, are just some of the questions I have been asked over the many years I have been researching the Louth Navigation. This book attempts to answer a few of the many questions people pose when looking around the canal's basin. This is a new history of The Louth Navigation. In it I have included new material and many corrections, along with page numbers and references which were absent from a previous book on the Navigation.

Josephine Clark contributed research on the Nell family, some additional material on the Chaplin family, the drinking houses and inns along the canal and the Social and Economic Development of the Riverhead in the nineteenth century.

We would like to thank Patricia Williams from New Zealand for her contribution on the history of the Nell Family, her ancestors. Finally we have to thank John Stanbridge, chairman of The Louth Navigation Trust, for editing this book.

We do hope you enjoy this new history.
Stuart Sizer.

CONTENTS

THE EARLY YEARS

In 1789 Richard Salmon, of Louth, wrote a poem about the town, part of which went:

> Indulgent Heaven, on this much favour'd Town,
> Has kindly poured its richest Blessings down;
> Good milk, good bread and wholesome home-brew'd Ale
> Fine springs of water never known to fail;
> Our markets well supply'd with Flesh and Fish;
> ....
> A bright example may this Town appear;
> Its Fame resound thro' ev'ry Village near;
> ....

And in 1799, the well known traveller, John Cragg visited Louth. His attention was drawn to the area once known as "Mallard Ings" and now called River Head, for here was the terminus of the Louth Navigation which was opened in 1770. Cragg wrote:

> ..." There seemed to be a deal of business done at it in coal, corn and wool carriage. The river basin is spacious and vessels of 50 tons burden come up it.....Saw a vessel building, their manner of driving and clenching the bolts I thought worth notice....Several warehouses for wool and granaries for wheat are built by the canal side, which looks like a town at a distance..."

These two extracts indicate that by the close of the eighteenth century Louth was a busy and prosperous town. It is quite obvious that the coming of the canal was turning the town into a rich and flourishing place in which to live.

The question is how was this achieved, when in his book "A History of Louth" the Rev. J. E. Swaby gave chapter 14 the title, "The Years of Sleep"? The years he referred to were between the middle of the 17th and 18th centuries. This period marked little change in the fortune of the town. In fact trade was at a virtual standstill. We were in danger of being left behind as the world outside Louth began to change with the beginnings of the Agrarian Revolution and later the Industrial Revolution further afield.

In the early 1750's the Warden and his Six Assistants (the mayor and council of the town, who had been created when Louth was granted its Charter in 1551) became increasingly concerned at the state of trade in the town and district. There was a general decline in business. It was extremely difficult to transport goods into or out of the town due to the poor state of the roads. For most of the year the roads, which in reality were no more than cart tracks, were virtually impassable. Many of these roads, or to be more accurate, tracks, simply followed the boundaries of the villages and fields they came too. The Corporation of the Town could see that Louth would continue to decline for lack of a satisfactory transport system.

It took a journey of two days, in good weather, for a cart loaded with wool or grain to reach the port of Grimsby, some 16 miles away. Here it could be loaded onto the Humber Keels or Sloops for transportation to the domestic worsted industry in Yorkshire. Goods could also be brought over from Hull and transported back to the Louth. But this was a slow process and not very economical.

The area around Louth was beginning to produce a surplus of wool and grain and there was a desperate need to find an alternative means of transportation. This was a direct result of the agrarian revolution. There was also the small matter of importing goods from the port of Hull, such as timber, coal and groceries. Coal at this time was for domestic use only.

ROADS

By the middle of the 18th century roads all over Britain were in such a state that in winter little or nothing could be transported without a great deal of time, money and effort being spent. Even then goods could only be moved slowly and not in great quantities. Roads were little more than mud tracks with deep ruts. It could take a horse and carriage more than three days to make the journey from Lincoln to Louth, a distance of 26 miles. Today we can make that journey in about 35 minutes. As we have seen the journey to the port of Grimsby could take two days. The route was not, as today, along the A16 but through South Elkington, Wold Newton, East Ravendale, Brigsley, Waltham and so to Grimsby. This route existed in 1765.

An engineer's report of the day stated that..." the land carriage of corn and wool is effected to the great detriment of trade and commerce because of the bad condition of the roads in wet seasons, whereby the cost of freight is greatly increased."

To move a cart loaded with corn just a few miles in winter would be almost impossible. It is hardly surprising that trade was just about at a standstill during the winter months.

In the summer things were little better. Provided the rutted roads had been ploughed and harrowed the warm weather would bake the surface and make them passable. Villages were supposed to take responsibility for the maintenance of the roads in and around their locality. Few parishes bothered to do much about them. In general there was little need for most of them to visit the next village or town.

Attempts to improve matters were made by the formation of "Turnpike Trusts". These Trusts levied a charge or toll for the passage of goods, carriages and animals along a stretch of road. The money collected in tolls was used to repair and improve roads. It was also used to build bridges over the many streams which crossed tracks.

Keddington Lock looking towards Louth

Keddington Lock c.1910

Footbridge at Alvingham Churches c.1910. Note the bridge swings to open for boats.

Fishing Cobble at Tetney Haven

In 1765 the Dexthorpe Trust attempted to improve the route to the west of Louth along the Elkington Road to Market Rasen and so to Bawtry. It passed through the town and along the present A16 to Dexthorpe just west of Ulceby Cross.

These Trusts did make a difference to the transportation system of the country. However, improvements were slow to come and there was a limit to what a horse and cart could carry. There was still a need for a more efficient means of transportation, particularly for the locally produced wool and corn.

In Ireland the Newry Canal, which had been opened in March 1742, was already being used for the transportation of goods. In 1755 the industrialists of St. Helens, in Lancashire, had just obtained an Act of Parliament for the construction of the Sankey Brook Navigation. It was opened in 1757 and goods could be transported along it to the River Mersey.

The areas served by the tidal rivers of the Humber, Trent and Yorkshire Ouse had little difficulty in expanding their trade using the traditional Humber Keels and Sloops of the area.

The port of Saltfleet, attached to the village of Skidbrook, had been in use since before the Norman times. During the middle ages much trade passed through this port on its way to and from Louth. Wool, cloth and wine were amongst the goods imported and exported via the Haven during the Middle Ages. No doubt coal was also landed here and at the several other ports along the coast. This can be seen by the number of Coal Shore Lanes along our coastline.

Was it possible for Louth to use a water transportation system as a solution to their problems? Louth had the River Lud. Could it be widened and extended to provide a solution to their problems? No doubt this scheme was considered by them. The Corporation decided to seek advice on the matter. They looked around for a suitable person who would be able to advise them.

The following map shows the waterway network to which the Louth canal ultimately had access. When the canal was first built it was to provide a relatively sheltered route by sea up the Humber to Hull, Grimsby as well as the East & West Riding & East Midland river network via the Ouse, Don, Aire and Trent. Subsequently many other canals were constructed such as the Sheffield & South Yorkshire Canal, the Calder & Hebble Navigation, and the Barnsley Canal. This gave Louth access to all the Yorkshire industrial cities, such as Bradford,, Doncaster, Leeds & Wakefield, predominantly textile cities; as well as Sheffield, the iron & steel capital of the country.

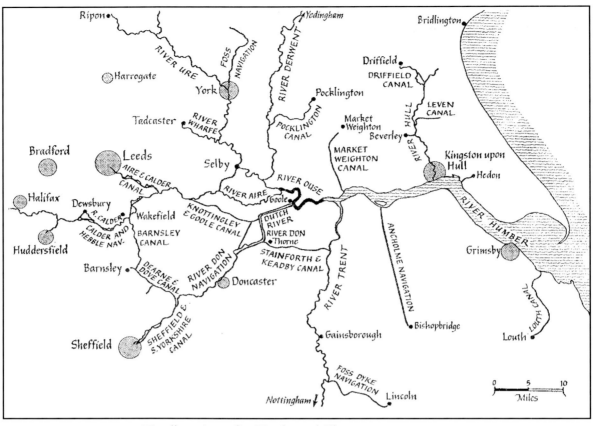

Trading Area for Keels and Sloops

JOHN GRUNDY

In October of 1756 they approached a Spalding engineer named John Grundy. John Grundy Junior (1719-1783) had been born in Market Bosworth, Leicestershire in 1719, the son of John Grundy Senior (1696-1748). He moved to Spalding with his parents on 27th December 1739.

Grundy Junior helped his father with surveys and the supervision of civil engineering works in Deeping Fen. They were responsible for the widening and straightening of rivers courses around the Wash and for the construction of sea sluices. Grundy junior learnt his skills in mathematics and other theoretical and practical skills from his father. These skills were to be put to good use in his career, as possibly, the first civil engineer to be trained in this country.

In 1738 Grundy Junior had been appointed Clerk and surveyor to the Company of Adventurers of Deeping. A year later he was admitted as a member of the Spalding Gentlemen's Society. In the same year he drew up a scheme, along with estimates, for the drainage of lowlands adjacent to the River Witham and for improving the navigation.

At this stage the Warden and Six thought Grundy was the ideal man to consult on the feasibility of a link between Louth and the sea. This was a confidence that was not to continue.

Grundy's brief was to explore the possibility of direct access by boats from Hull, and other ports along the Humber and its tributaries to the town of Louth. Grundy knew the town was on the eastern edge of the Wolds, where the little river Lud emerged from the hills and wound its way to Alvingham, where it lost itself in the many streams which wandered the 8 miles to the coast.

There were a number of ports along this stretch of coastline. The main ones were at Saltfleet, Tetney and Grimsby, along with smaller ports at Grainthorpe and Somercotes. It was with this brief that Grundy set about surveying a possible route in October 1756.

THE ROUTE

A link to the sea via a widened River Lud and a man-made waterway to Saltfleet were quickly cast aside as the sea journey from the exposed waters of the North Sea to the more sheltered Humber was considered too dangerous for the flat bottomed Sloops that would have to use it. Winter storms could quite easily turn the ships over or the high winds snap the mast if the sail could not be got down quickly. The ships were normally manned by two men.

Another consideration was the course of the River Lud from Louth to Alvingham. It was far too winding to be used even if it could be widened. A different route would have to be found. This was not a difficult task for Grundy as the Marsh to the northeast of Louth was flat and low lying. This would save having to construct too many expensive locks.

After his initial survey Grundy proposed a route from Louth, following the course of the little River Lud, to the north of Alvingham. From there it was to turn northwards, across Grainthorpe Fen, Wragholme Ings, Fulstow Ings, Thoresby Fen, and so to Tetney and its little port. This meant access to the River Humber could be gained without having to spend much time in the dangerous German Ocean, as the North Sea was then known.

Grundy proposed to construct a sea sluice and lock at the Port of Tetney. The entrance to the Humber would require straightening by way of a new sea cut to avoid the tortuous meanders of the haven. There would be a further 9 locks required before the navigation reached Louth some twelve miles away. However, these locks would be in the upper half of the route between Alvingham and Louth. The proposed terminus of the Navigation would be at the eastern limit of the town, close to the present War Memorial.

The lower part of the proposed navigation would, like the vast majority of Grundy's schemes, assist in land drainage. It was, he suggested, an important factor in helping to persuade the owners of the land the canal would have to cross.

In his report to the Corporation Grundy outlined the advantages of the scheme as:

> "..keeping the cut at all times two feet lower than the lowest surface of the land adjacent to it, and therefore assist in its drainage, and that the sea sluice being to the limit of that height would, therefore, allow sufficient fall to perfect drainage of those lands".

From the sluice and lock at Tetney, there would be no need for any more locks until the canal reached Alvingham Fen, seven miles inland, thus saving money. The land owners would be compensated, in full, for the land they were likely to loose due to the cut.

Grundy proposed wagon, horse and foot bridges should be built, wherever necessary.

Where a water course crossed the proposed navigation, sluices were to be built to assist with drainage. However, if a landowner wished the water course to continue he proposed the construction of a 'subterraneous tunnel' under the canal, a further carrot to the land owners.

It was suggested that land in and around North Coates, Marsh Chapel and Grainthorpe could be watered by the canal in periods of drought. This could be achieved by raising the water level at Tetney thus providing the land owners with an irrigation scheme. The reverse of the drainage of land already proposed.

In part of his report he wrote:

> ".....the nearest ports or harbours to Louth are Saltfleet, Tetney, and Grimsby from whence it is supply'd with coals, deals, groceries etc. and to which a great part of the corn, wool and other produce is convey'd by land carriage for Exportation. The country through which this land carriage is performed being mostly flat drowned marshes, the soil a strong clay, and the roads in the wet season so deep, founderous, and bad that it is with the greatest difficulty and at an immense expense that this land carriage is effected to the great detriment of Trade and Commerce and to the great hurt and disadvantage of the Landed Interest of all the country adjoining."

Grundy's report, sent to the Corporation in early 1757, confirmed what they had suspected. A Navigation from Louth to Tetney Haven appeared feasible. Thus a route by water was to be built to the port of Tetney to improve the existing links by road. In April 1757 Grundy was paid £30 16s 9 d for his report, survey and estimate.

His report lists the costs for the construction of a navigation as:

Canal wide enough for 2 barges	Canal for 1 barge + passing places	For Lighters only

From Tetney Haven to the New Bridge in Louth.

£15,590	£13,686	£10,884

From Tetney Haven to the Meadow below the Leather Mill.

£12,968	£11,241	£8,931

Mill near Louth.

From Tetney Haven to the old mill, Keddington.

£11,098	£9,481	£7,589

From Tetney Haven to the Top of Alvingham Out Fen.

£7,853	£6,566	£5,312

A Lighter was a craft which was towed by horse on inland river systems.

The estimates shown above did not include the cost of obtaining the Act and a full survey. Grundy estimated that marsh land would cost around £10 per acre and meadow £20 per acre. The canal was to be 1 1³/₄ miles in length with ten locks, including the sea lock and sluice at Tetney. The total fall of water between Louth and Tetney was calculated to be 43' 9".

Whether the projected cost of between £8,931 and £15,590 to bring the Navigation to Louth put the Corporation, and those interested, off the scheme, is not clear. It is quite possible that the large sum involved, some £660,000 to around £1,000,000 in today's money, came as a shock to the Warden and his Assistants and their backers. For a small market town like Louth already in recession it would have seemed an almost impossible sum to raise.

From the commissioning of the report in 1756 to the next move in the story of the Navigation was a matter of four years. During which several things nationally had taken place. The Sankey Brook, or St. Helens Canal as it became known, was constructed. A start was made to the, now famous, Bridgewater Canal by James Brindley, which was opened in 1761, and John Smeaton was making a name for himself as an engineer and canal builder.

THE FIRST ACT (1763)

The Corporation had to work hard before there was enough interest for a subscription to be opened towards the costs of the Act and a full survey. However, by the 28th January 1760 there was enough interest being shown for the scheme to move forwards. The Town's poor economic position had no doubt played a part in this. The money to be raised was required to pay for a proper Survey and obtaining the Act of Parliament not the construction of the Navigation.

Minutes of a General Meeting of those interested records the Corporation, through its Warden John Cravoft, gave £100 towards the costs. The amounts from other subscribers varied between £10 and £50. The Subscribers had now raised £870.

At a further meeting held on the 18th February attended by John Cravoft, his assistants D. Atkinson, Thomas Hardy, C. Clark and W. Willerton, the High Steward J Birch and seven other citizens of Louth, it was decided to ask the Town Clerk, Sam Towmaw, to write to Mr. John Smeaton, who was by this time gaining a reputation as an engineer living in Holborn, London, asking him to go over Grundy's proposals in relation to costs, levels and any other advice he could offer.

He wrote:

> 'The Gentlemen of the Corporation of the Town of Louth, apprehending it to be practicable that a Navigable River may be made from the River Humber to the town of Louth desire your assistance in taking levels of the course of the intended river, computing the charge of making the same, and your advice upon the whole. They are desirous of being forward in their undertaking as possible and desire the favour of you (in case it is convenient for you to attend the business) to come to Louth as soon as possible as you can.'

Smeaton replied on the 23rd stating he intended to spend the summer in the north and was pretty busy and could not say how far he would be able to assist them. However, he did ask for more details of the scheme. He added a rather shrewd postscript:

"PS. Is the expense and practicability the chief point, or rather the getting the Bill through Parliament on account of an expected opposition?"

His letter was discussed at a meeting held on the 28th. It was decided to sent him a further letter saying the proposed navigation was intended to follow the River (Lud) for about 4 miles to Alvingham and then make a new cut about 8 miles long to the Humber at Tetney Haven. They went on to say that not much opposition was expected and it was hoped to introduce a Bill into the next session of Parliament. A survey, considered practicable, had already been made by Mr Grundy. However they were not prepared to proceed with the scheme without further opinion.

Smeaton replied on the 11th March saying that providing not all the works he was engaged in were in progress he would be in Louth during the summer. In his letter Smeaton gave very wise advice on the need to go slowly. He also went on to say how extremely busy he was and that he did not wish the Corporation to delay their application because of him.

He advised them to make the scheme known publicly as soon as possible to the people of the town. He also advised that they should gain the consent of the majority of the landowners along the proposed navigation as opposition had a way of showing itself only after the petition had been presented to Parliament.

A further letter was sent to Smeaton asking him to give a definite answer. He replied in late June saying he hoped to be in the town in about a month's time. A reply was sent to Smeaton on 28th July requesting him to fix his own time to meet with John Grundy.

It appears even at this early stage in the planning, the Warden and Six and their backers did not altogether believe John Grundy was capable of carrying out the project. Perhaps it was more to do with the fact that Grundy had only been concerned with widening rivers and the construction of sea sluices and new sea cuts rather than the construction of canals.

On the 7th August a meeting was held in the Town Hall, which used to stand in Mercer Row opposite Woolworth. It was attended by the Warden, Charles Clarke, his assistants Nicholas Wrigglesworth, W. Willerton and Thomas Hardy and fourteen subscribers. Here they elected a secretary, Thomas Knight at a rate of 3/4d for every attendance, and two treasurers, Messrs Bealey and Willerton. A minute was passed asking for a further 10% of the sums previously subscribed to be collected from each member and paid to the treasurers.

Smeaton and Grundy first met, on the 17th August 1760, at the Blue Stone Inn in Upgate, Louth. There, they went over Grundy's report. Smeaton broadly agreed with Grundy and his formal report contained only a few minor alterations, one of which was to the proposed route, which he thought might be helpful.

At a further meeting of the promoters, held on the 23rd, August, it was minuted that any seven subscribers attending a meeting would constitute a committee and that they had the authority to call further meetings and carry out any business found necessary for the smooth running of the Navigation.

In September of 1760 John Grundy along with Dr Clarke and Dr Hardy, who were members of the promoters of the canal, attended Lincoln races. The idea was to gain support from the County's nobility and gentry for the scheme. At that time the backing of the wealthy landed classes was essential. They would give respectability to a scheme and also, hopefully, financial support. They dominated parliament then and could be helpful if it was necessary to pass an act of parliament. The three men came away from the races with a feeling of satisfaction.

On the 15th September the Promoters discussed the feedback they had received. The Duke of Ancaster had listened to the scheme and thought it useful for the public good. William Banks Esq. of Revesby thought the scheme a useful one and was prepared to assist. He also made several suggestions for the promoters to consider relating to land in Marshchapel and Fulstow. He also suggested that the present water course from the blow-wells at Tetney should be retained.

Lord Scarborough suggested the landowners should be approached before the Bill was presented to Parliament and Lord Monson requested he be sent more details of the scheme. At a later interview the subscribers were given the support of Charles Pelham of Brocklesby, a member of the Yarborough family, owning land in North Lincolnshire. Many more people were interviewed and the vast majority were in favour of the scheme.

John Chaplin Esq., a wealthy gentleman landowner, who lived at Tathwell, just outside Louth, thought the Navigation was bound to be of great benefit to the people of Louth and district. He promised to do all in his power to help promote the scheme. His son, Charles Chaplin, was later to become a major shareholder and obtained the lease on the tolls of the Navigation. The Chaplin family had a controlling interest in the navigation from 1770 until the coming of the railways in the 1840s.

One voice of dissent was that of a Captain Clayton. He declared he had little property that would be of benefit to him and that he had much more that might cause hurt so he hoped the petition would fail.

Robert Vyner Esq. foresaw much opposition from the people of Grimsby. He advised the promoters to organise a meeting with them to explain their proposals.

These suggestions and requests were quickly acted upon, for by the 25th September it had been agreed that a letter be circulated to the landowners. A meeting had taken place with Mr Christopher Clayton, the Mayor of Grimsby. He had been made familiar with the scheme. He had been asked to call a meeting of the Corporation to discuss their proposals as soon as possible. This he agreed to do. One leading citizen of Grimsby, Captain Spenlove thought the scheme a useful one.

It was further reported that all the Grimsby people interviewed had expressed a view that there should be a Turnpike between Louth and their town. A Turnpike Act was passed in 1765.

On the 3rd October the treasurer was asked to pay Drs. Hardy and Clarke and Mr Wrigglesworth £7-15-9d as payment for expenses incurred during their travels.

After further correspondence in early 1761 between Grundy and Smeaton the committee were informed that they were:

> "United in opinion for carrying on the Navigation".

At this time the land owners at Tetney were worried about the drainage scheme being proposed. John Smeaton wrote to Grundy pointing out that the people of Tetney should be grateful for the provision of a free sea sluice. He went on to say that if they continued to cause trouble a new route via the North Cotes Fleet could be used, thus avoiding Tetney altogether. Grundy disagreed with this proposal saying the Fleet was too shallow in the dry season. Their letters show a respect for one another's views and abilities despite their differences.

By September of 1761 meetings were still being held to try and speed up the sending of reports to the various landowners along the proposed route of the Navigation. The treasurer was asked to pay £12-15-0 to Mr Parker for printing these plans.

On the 24th November 1761 it was decided to call a General Meeting of the subscribers which was to be held in the Town Hall in Louth at which any objectors could attend. This meeting was to take place on 31st December and advertisements were to be place in the Stamford Mercury, the General Evening Post and the London Chronicle. The Promoters said that they intended to introduce the Bill in the next session of Parliament (1762/63).

The meeting was well attended and included the Right Honourable, the Earl of Scarborough, Ayscough Boucherett Esq. Nicholas Wrigglesworth Esq. Warden of Louth, John Maddison Esq. and many others. The reports of Smeaton and Grundy along with the heads of the Bill were read out and approved by all present.

By this time several more clauses had been added to the 32 already in the Draft Bill. By July 1762 it was agreed a petition should be drawn up asking leave to bring the Bill before Parliament. A Mr Yates was given this task. It was sent to Nottingham to be printed in October 1762.

 A further general meeting was fixed for 10 am on the 22nd July 1762 to be held in the Mansion House in Upgate, Louth. Once again advertisements were to be place advertising this.

On July 15th a meeting was held to appoint a new secretary following the death of Thomas Knight Esq. George Jolland was elected to fill the vacancy at the rate of 3/4d per meeting attended.

This meeting was once again well attended. It included the Earl of Scarborough, George and Winfer Heneage, Samuel Mastin, together with six vicars. The Heads of the Bill were discussed and altered and approved.

On the following day it was proposed that the amended heads of the Bill be sent to the printers and distributed to those concerned with the navigation. The secretary was asked to draw up a Petition to be presented to Parliament for leave to bring up the said Bill. That the said Petition be presented at the beginning of the next session of Parliament. They appointed Mr Yates to draw up the Bill.

On the 18th November it was proposed that Captain Floyer should go to London with instructions for Council concerning the drawing up of a Bill. He was to "advise and consult" with anyone there who might help in speeding up the passage through Parliament. He was to be allowed expenses for liquor etc. for any meeting he had to attend! The petition was presented to Parliament on the 6th December, 1762. Both Grundy and Smeaton gave the scheme their support.

At a meeting of the Committee held on the 20th January 1763 in the Blue Stone public house in Upgate objections were read out from the people of Tetney. They were concerned about the propose route and suggested the Navigation take a more westerly line in Tetney Common so as to come within half a mile of the village. They claimed the ground there was two feet lower than the proposed route, and that the soil there was of less value than the proposed route and would provide better drainage for the low land in Tetney.

The committee asked Mr Grundy to look into these proposals and report back to them. At a subsequent meeting Grundy reported that the people had misunderstood his plans, placing the Navigation more to the east than was actually intended. He went on to say that he could make an alteration which would mean cutting a further 6 chains (around 600 feet) along the boundary dyke between Thoresby Fen and Mr Sibthorpe's Close. By this route the proposed tunnel under North Cotes Fleet would not be required. He estimated the additional cost to be £25.

Mr Grundy went on to criticise a route which had been pegged out, most likely by the people of Tetney, as wrong and would go against all the principles of drainage.

At the same meeting Captain Floyer was asked to attend Parliament to promote the Bill. He was also to use Mr Grundy and Mr Smeaton in the Commons or Lords to help with any technical details. All expenses were to be reimbursed.

On 14th February Captain Floyer requested a sum of £100 to help him force the Bill along without loss of any more time. This sounds like a little bribery was required! The request was agreed and subscribers were asked for a further advance of 10%. Everyone had done their job well for the Bill was passed on the 24th March 1763.

On the 5th April 1763 the secretary placed an advertisement in the Stamford Mercury stating that an Act of Parliament had been passed and that the Committee responsible were to meet at the Blue Stone. All subscribers were to attend for the settling of accounts and "all persons to bring in their bills".

FINANCES

The Act did not provide funds for the construction of the canal. What it did was to empower the newly appointed Board of Commissioners to raise moneys against the anticipated tolls.

In May 1763 a notice was posted out in Louth, Caistor, Horncastle and Market Rasen stating that the Commissioners of the Louth Navigation wished to borrow money from any person wishing to lend. They also placed adverts in the General Evening Post, the York Courrant, the Cambridge Journal and the Stamford Mercury requesting the same.

At this time the Earl of Scarborough was elected a Commissioner in place of W. Williamson who had died and was named in the Act.

A further advert was printed on 19th July 1764 stating that £12,000 was necessary to carry out the works of the Navigation and this sum was to be raised by the sale of transferable shares of £100 each. Any person wishing to lend should contact Mr Jolland.

On the 20th September 1764 a list of subscribers was drawn up and makes interesting reading. Of the thirty-two subscribers listed the Earl of Scarborough held thirty shares worth £3,000. However, a minute of the Commissioners stated that no single person should hold more than £2,000's worth! No amendment to the minute has been found. Later the Earl was elected a commissioner himself. The Earl's involvement would, no doubt, encourage others to subscribe to the scheme. It would have been deemed a small matter to break the Commissioners own rules in such circumstances.

Among other subscribers were; Charles Chaplin - 10 shares worth £1,000, A Boucherett - 10 shares worth £1,000, William Floyer - 10 shares again worth £1,000, W. Marshall - 5 shares worth £500 and Charles Clarke with 2 shares worth £200.

During the final months of 1764 the Commissioners held several meetings but all were adjourned because of poor attendance by the Commissioners.

However, on 25th January 1765 the Commissioners offered John Grundy the post of supervisor for the construction of the Navigation and to appoint an inspector for the carrying out the works.

On 11th February the Commissioners appointed Charles Chaplin Esq. as Treasurer, and on 13th February Robert Morton replaced William Willerton, who had died, as a Commissioner. Notice was served to the Lords of the Manors of Tetney, Fulstow and North Thoresby, and to the various landowners that the Commissioners for the Navigation wished to meet to discuss terms for the land which was to be cut. Captain Floyer, William Gilliatt and William Smith of Hatcliffe, who was an Enclosure Commissioner for Holton-le-Clay and Rothwell, went to value land at Tetney.

The result of their valuation of the land was:

Tetney Common and waste:

> For land to be cut 10 guineas per acre.
> For the land to be covered 5 guineas per acre.

Fitty ground (salt marsh)
Land to be cut 30 shillings per acre or a rent charge of 12 pence per acre, per annum.
> Land covered 15 shillings per acre or 6d per acre per annum.

Smalldrain Close, North Cotes:

> Land to be cut £6 per acre.
> Land to be covered £3 per acre.

The same valuation was placed on North Thoresby Common. All the valuations were confirmed by contract on the 27 June.

It had been eight and a half years since Grundy had first been approached regarding the possibility of a Navigation. Had the scheme gone ahead earlier it could well have been in the History Books as the 'First Canal' in the new age rather than the Sankey Brook or the more well known Bridgewater Canal.

CONSTRUCTION

With the promise of money construction could now begin. At a meeting of the Commissioners, held on the 11th February 1765, Mr. John Grundy was appointed the engineer for the project. On 14th March Grundy appointed James Hogard as his supervisor of works. It may be that Hogard was a relative of Thomas Hogard who had worked on the Deeping Fen project in 1764. James Hogard later became the collector of tolls for the navigation. To get things underway as quickly as possible the Commissioners requested Grundy send his sailing barge from Spalding to Tetney with barrows and planks for a hundred men. This gives us a clear indication of the number of men to be employed on the construction of the Navigation.

It should be remembered that the Commissioners first offered the post of engineer to John Smeaton in January of 1765. However, Smeaton declined the offer as he had other projects to manage. Grundy was the Commissioners second choice as engineer, which may explain the Commissioners' subsequent behaviour towards him.

Work began at Tetney Haven to construct the lock, sea sluice and the sea cut early in 1765. The lock and sea sluice had to control the tidal waters of Tetney Haven as well as the depth of water in the canal. Straightening Tetney Haven was necessary as the estuary was far from straight and would prove extremely difficult for the keels, sloops and other vessels to navigate. Grundy's plan quite clearly shows what had to be done. Evidence from present-day aerial views confirms this.

A problem arose at this point between Mr Grundy and Messrs Pindar and Harrison of Tetney over the sale of land. They said they were unable to discuss the sale of land when they did not know to which land Mr Grundy was referring, for it had not been marked out. One supposes Grundy thought that as the price for land to be cut had been agreed there was no need to specify which section of land he required. The clerk to the Commissioners interceded with the owners and work commenced. No doubt this problem only served to reinforce in the Commissioners their feeling of dissatisfaction with Grundy over his management of the project.

It was at this time that the decision was taken to construct the canal so two ships could pass each other without the need for passing bays having to be constructed. It meant the navigation would cost around £16,000.

Large numbers of workmen would be employed in the canal's construction, many of them of Irish origin. After the canal's completion a number stayed on in the town with some living in Trinity Lane and others in cottages on Irish Hill which is off the west end of Westgate, hence the name. Others were farm labourers who had been thrown out of work by the enclosures of the eighteenth century. Some were Scottish labourers who could not find work in their own country. These men were known originally as 'cutters'. However, by the 1790's they had become known as 'navigators', which later became shortened to 'navvies'.

Every bit of earth had to be removed by picks, spades, shovels and wheelbarrows and the sweat and toil of the navvies. Timber for the bridges and lock gates was sawn by hand using pit saws and manpower only. The iron work required would have been forged by local blacksmiths. The bricks for the lock walls were hand made on site or where suitable clay had been found.

An early engraving of Keddington lock (P.5) shows the balance beams of the lock gates to be the trunks of trees. One can assume from this that the majority, if not all beams, would have been the same. The balance beam is the section of the lock gate or swing-bridge which is used to open and close the gate. Later photographs show the tree trunks to have been replaced by cut timbers.

The lock pit floors were covered with transverse and lateral timbers placed on timber piers embedded in the clay (P. 26). This would lead to problems at a later stage with the timbers by the upper gates and sill. The timbers there would suffer from the constant fall of water when the pit was being filled or the flow of water over topped the gates. Eventually some would be displaced or simply rotted and scouring would take place causing the walls to lean towards one another.

The handmade bricks were laid straight onto the large timbers and not as first thought onto the clay bed. This was confirmed when the Louth Navigation Trust carried out remedial work in 1997 to stop further deterioration of Ticklepenny Lock.

A minute of the Canal Commissioners of 13 February 1765 shows that enquiries were to be made at Tetney, and elsewhere, regarding the purchase of 300,000 bricks.

On 10th April the Commissioners asked for a survey of land as far as Fire Beacon Lane be carried out in readiness for the purchase and later development. The following month saw the Commissioners issuing a statement claiming that they were now ready to meet with the owners of the land with a view to purchasing it.

The Commissioners requested that Mr Knott, who was one of Grundy's agents, should inspect the condition of the barrows and planks which Grundy had sent from Spalding. He was required to report to the Commissioners fortnightly.

A survey was now carried out on the land between Fire Beacon Lane and the upper end of Alvingham Out Fen. The construction of a canal was a complex matter requiring a great deal of forward planning and good management. As digging took place on one section the land ahead had to be surveyed and marked out. Beyond that negotiations took place for the purchase of the land.

On the 28th August Mr Grundy was urged by the Commissioners to "expedite the work of His Navigation". Mr Grundy was asked to appear before the Commissioners on 5th September as they suspected him of misplacing or losing materials. He was able to show that the materials had never arrived and was completely cleared of all charges. They told him to purchase the necessary equipment from Hull for the construction of the sluice.

In another minute of a meeting held on the 10th October 1765 in the Mansion House Mr Grundy was told to pay Mr. John Ludlam £52 10s 0d for 60,000 bricks at 17s 6d per 1,000 and for 500 more which had been delivered to the Sluice Pit at Tetney Haven. James Hogard was appointed as Collector of Tolls of 4d. per ton per mile at this time. A proportionate toll was to be levied on vessels between Tetney Haven and the Sluice.

By the middle of November of that year Joseph Cook of Barton upon Humber, a bricklayer, had been contracted to lay bricks for the sea sluice and lock at a rate of 23shillings per rod (16/18 feet). His contract was to be between March and Mayday 1766.

He reported he had found suitable clay for brick making. Cook was also contracted to produce some 400,000 bricks, 9" x 4½" x 2¼" on Tetney Common at a price of 11shillings per thousand. He also had to provide his own planks, barrows and tables. At the same time Frederick Soate was contracted to produce 400,000 bricks of the same size near Alvingham. Presumably they were for the building of the locks and bridges there.

In the following year a contract was awarded to Mr Frederick L'Oste, who had previously been a Commissioner but had now waived that position, to supply 400,000 bricks at Alvingham. The price was to be 13/6d per 1,000. Cook and Soate had been offered 11s per 1,000. There is no explanation for the discrepancy in price, as in both cases, all the materials were available at the sites and the specifications were the same. It is quite probable that L'Oste was benefiting from his previous position as a Commissioner.

On the 10th December the Commissioners gave William Sowden, a tenant of William Tathwell, notice for the purchase of some of his close at Alvingham for brick making.

James Hoggard produced a survey of the land for cutting from Fire Beacon Lane to the middle of Grainthorpe Fen. This was followed by a notice to the owners or their tenants of that land. Contracts were drawn up with Messrs Walesby, Tuxworth, Wilkinson and Leafe, and the Reverends Tyson, Bradley, Holland and Wadeson for the purchase of their lands. Prices were to be fixed by Messrs. Gilliatt and Smith.

In February of 1766 Mr Grundy provided a horse-mill, to help with drainage of the water. He was also asked to provide two lighters of about four tons for carrying materials along the cut. In the following month there was an advert placed in the Cambridge Journal and the Stamford Mercury for a bricklayer, to construct the horse bridges along the canal between Tetney and Alvingham. The work was to commence in mid summer 1766.

In March the Commissioners sent a warning to William Thistleton saying that the brick-layers were waiting to move on to the site "and if he does not immediately perform his works on the Grand Sluice, he will incur the displeasure of the Commissioners". They were not prepared to accept excuses and they fully intended to offer the work to someone else! So he had better pull his finger out as the saying goes.

On the 7th June Grundy sent a letter to the Commissioners explaining that he had persuaded Messrs. Bennett and Thistleton to build two wagon-bridges at £100 each. This included materials and carriage. The costs allowed were:

> £24-15-0 for bricks
> £1-13-4 for old barrow-planks for the foundations.
> £1-16-0 for the Riga timber for the coping.

A horse bridge was to be built on Landyke bank at a cost of £44. This bank was the main route between the villages of Fulstow and Marshchapel. It was proposed to send the materials by barge so the water was to be retained until all the materials had been delivered.

By late June, 1766 the sea sluice was completed. The sluice had doors pointing to sea. When the tide came in the pressure of water closed then. As the tide went out the doors would open as surplus water from the canal flowed out to sea. Behind the doors were the draw doors which could be adjusted in height. These served an additional purpose in that not only controlling the depth of water in the canal but when drawn up would help to scour out the channel to seaward. The lock had two sets of doors one set pointing to sea and the other set pointing to land.

In a minute of 26th June it was recorded that Mr Grundy's contract of employment would end on the 11th August, 1766. There has been speculation that there were irregularities with the canal finances at the time. However, Grundy went on to other projects. It is inconceivable that he would have been employed by others had the allegations been true. A more likely answer may be found from extracts in the minutes. There appears to have been engineering and other problems, which may have led to the termination of Mr Grundy's contract. The minutes show that several bridges were too narrow. The quantity of bricks required was too small and the brickmaker was given permission to exceed the stated quantity.

Another problem encountered at that time, which may have added to the Commissioners resolve to dispense with Grundy's services was with Thoresby Fen Bridge, built by Messrs Bennett & Thistleton. The bridge was found to be: "insufficient and part of it was down". Perhaps Grundy was thought not to have supervised well enough for the liking of the Commissioners. It is quite obvious that some or all of the Commissioners did not trust Grundy.

The bridge that was eventually built at Thoresby Fen was only one of two which was fixed, the other being Alvingham High Bridge. All the rest were swing bridges of varying sizes according to the type of transport using them. Thoresby Bridge was a carriage bridge. The height from the surface of the water to the underside of the arch was 10 feet 3 inches. Its width at the waters surface was 22 feet 6 inches, of which 5 feet was taken up for a towing path.

Grundy's agent for the project was James Hogard. It would be Hogard who managed the day to day supervision of the men and construction work. Hogard succeeded Grundy as supervisor/engineer after his dismissal, but his appointment was not confirmed until 18th May 1767, perhaps he was on trial for a period.

It was on the same day, in 1767, that an advertisement appeared in the Stamford Mercury, York Courrant and Cambridge Journal reporting that the canal was to be opened from Tetney Haven to Fire Beacon Lane, a distance of about 7 miles. That stretch of canal had taken around two years to complete, not a bad achievement considering they had to work through two winters.

By this time it was evident that the Commissioners were running out of money and the original estimate of over £14,000 was totally inadequate. In May of 1767 a subscription of £5,000 was opened. And in May 1768 a further £2,400 was required to complete the works. This money was to be raised by the Subscribers themselves and any one else wishing to join them. In actual fact, an extra £14,000 was required before the canal was completed, bringing the total cost for constructing the navigation to around £28,000, a considerable sum of money in those days and well over £2,000,000 by today's standards.

A list of subscribers from the 18th May 1767 were:

	£
Charles Chaplin for Lady Elizabeth Chaplin	1,000
The Earl of Scarborough	600
Charles Chaplin	500
William Floyer	200
B. Bennett	200
Nicholas Wrigglesworth	200
Joseph L'Oste	200
W. Allenby	100
I Dawson	100
A Boucherett	500
William Welby	100
Richard Wharfe	200
Francis Willerton	400
John Wood	200
John Storr	100
Charles Clarke, Warden of Louth	1,000
Godfrey Outram	100
Robert Fatchit	100
H Andrews	100
Geofrey Barton and Elizabeth Trollop	200
Arthur Pearson	100
Sarah Pettener	500
William Floyer for Robert Yeates Esq.	500
Rev. J. Goodwin for the Rev. F. Sugar	100
A Boucherette Esq. from 24th June 1769	200
	£7,700

During that May it was decided a horse bridge should be built at Biergate Lane, and a waggon bridge at Fire Beacon Lane. It was also reported that the canal had been vandalised, between Tetney and Fire Beacon, by "persons unknown". A five guinea reward was offered for any information regarding the incidents.

Construction continued from Fire Beacon to Louth. Between July and November of 1768 over half a million bricks were ordered. As the canal approached Louth more locks were required as the ground began to rise, hence the large quantity needed. Work got underway on constructing the locks, sluices and bridges along the final section of the canal.

Mr Hogard was instructed to build a house at Tetney Sluice, presumably for the Lock Keeper. It was at this time that Mr Grundy's links with the Navigation was finally broken when his bill was settled and he received a final sum of £173 - 1 - 7¾d

In August the first goods were carried along the newly opened section of canal from Tetney to Fire Beacon. Ten vessels of coal ordered by Mr Wrigglesworth, a commissioner, from a Mr W. Hurst were transported to Fire Beacon.

The Clerk to the Commissioners had to write to William Ellinson, of Thorne in Yorkshire, stating that his servant (captain?) Isaac Wildbone, had run his keel into a boat belonging to the Navigation, laid up in a passing place and had staved in a gunwhale, hull and two planks, to the cost of £1-4-4d. The Commissioners expected him to make good the amount if he was to avoid prosecution.

Around July a contract was made with William Dunn for 150,000 bricks, "to be well burnt, good and merchantable". They were to be of the standard size, 9"x 4½" x 2¼". The brick close was at Louth, and the bricks were to be delivered at regular intervals between the present time and Martinmas week, around the 11th November. It was to be cash on delivery at 14shillings per thousand.

As the canal approached Alvingham Messrs Welfitt and Bennett were sent to survey land belonging to Mr Maddison in that village with a view to purchase. However, Maddison disagreed with the price of £155 being offered and exercised his right to be assessed by jury.

After visits to the site and due consideration the jury awarded Maddison £162 - 0 - 3½d for the land. However after expenses for summoning the jury and for taking them to Alvingham and back, the inquest came to £41 - 12 - 6d. Maddison was left with £120 - 7 - 9d, a loss on the initial assessment of £34 - 12 - 2¾d. The Commissioners possibly felt this just reward for all the trouble Maddison had caused.

Whilst all this was going on lock dues for tiles were fixed at 4 shillings per thousand. A committee was formed from the Commissioners on the 3rd November 1768 to contract with Frederick L'Oste and Edward Gray for 500,000 bricks. The Commissioners said that they would find the soil for clay at or near Louth. The two were "to dig, mould, set and burn the same." The bricks were to be of standard size. They were to be stacked in blocks of 1,000. The prices were fixed at:

Good	13s – 6d per 1,000
Fair	12s – 0d per 1,000
Rejected	1s -0d per 1,000 for the cost of the clay.

They wished the work to commence from the spring and were to be completed as soon as possible in the summer. Payment was to be half the amount fixed for half the number completed.

In February 1769 it was decided to construct a bridge at Keddington End, now close to Willows' Lock.

During this time there were several accidents to bridges or wharves caused by barges running into them. A Robert Gilderdale wrote to the Commissioners admitting that his sloop had damaged the lock at Alvingham. Gilderdale paid £16 as a deposit for the repairs.

In September of 1769 Hogard and Newark Cuthbert were asked to establish the cost of roads to Mallard Ings. It had also been decided to build a road on the north side of the basin.

Later in September a meeting of the Commissioners decided that work should commence on the new road to the Riverhead and they appointed Dr Clarke, Mr Wrigglesworth and Richard Wharfe to superintend the work.

A little after this a meeting of the Commissioners, held at the New King's Head in Mercer Row, decided to draw up a contract with the Warden and his assistants of Louth for the purchase of the land called Mallard's Ings. The soil belonged to the Corporation, and the common rights, after the crop of hay had been removed, belonged to the inhabitants of Louth.

At a meeting held on the 20th December 1769, the Commissioners decided that Mr Hubbard should have the right to use the water at Riverhead for his mill. It was to be maintained at his own expense, on condition that the Navigation would not in any way be obstructed or damaged.

It was decided that the canal was to terminate at the place known as Mallard Ings, about a mile east of the town, and not as originally intended in Ramsgate, near to the War Memorial. This new site for the canal basin saved about half a mile of canal, and two expensive locks.

On the 20th January 1770 the Commissioners let the tolls of the Navigation to Mr Charles Chaplin for a seven year period at a rent of 4% per annum.

The canal finally opened in May 1770, it was eleven and three quarter miles in length, and contained eight locks including the sea lock at Tetney. There would have been great celebrations at the time and, no doubt, a certain relief on the part of the Commissioners and Subscribers alike. There would be the anticipation of the trade the canal would bring, and the wealth to be made from the passage of goods.

THE LOCKS

Possibly the most interesting feature of the canal is the shape of the top six locks. Instead of having the standard parallel sides they were constructed with four segmented or 'barrel' shaped arches, which curved into the land. At the springing point of each arch there were wooden land ties. This suggests an attempt being made to strengthen the lock sides against the pressures of the surrounding land which was boulder clay and as the locks themselves had to be wider than normal to take the Humber Keels and Sloops which were to use the navigation. These ships, whenever possible, sailed up the navigation to save the cost of hiring a horse which would be used to tow them.

It is not really known who designed these arched or 'barrel' locks, whether Hogard used Grundy's design or thought of them himself. They may even have been part of the improvements suggested by Smeaton, using his knowledge gained in designing and building the third Eddystone lighthouse. Whoever may have designed them they are an unusual feature in this country and at the time of construction was unique.

The construction of the locks deserves consideration. Firstly the site of the lock was carefully chosen and pegged out. Then the navvies moved in. They dug out the lock chamber. This was made larger than the actual lock was to be. Piles were driven into the chamber floor and levelled, forming a supporting platform for the timbers.

The main wall timbers were laid on the outside piles with cross and lateral timbers being added. These wall timbers were of considerable width for they had to support the bricks which formed the lock walls and were of oak. At the springing points of the barrel locks a tie beam was added. This was added to give the lock walls additional strength. Once the brickwork was completed the earth was back filled and compacted. Capping stones, iron work and gates were then added.

From the evidence of Padley's report of 1828 this initial work to strengthen the locks was not altogether successful. Alvingham lock was found to be in a poor state of repair. Padley reported that the lock walls were overhanging their foundations upwards of two feet. He also reported that Salter Fen Lock was getting weak and would soon be ruinous.

Another interesting point about the canal is that no two locks are of the same dimensions. For example, what we now call 'Willows' Lock has a length of 85' 11", while Tetney's is 100'. The lock at Keddington is 15' 3" wide, while at Austin Fen it is 19'. The depth of water in the canal was to be 5' 4" over the sill. This was necessary because of the type of vessel using the canal.

Grundy's original plan and elevation for the construction of a lock

Lock Pit repair in 1995 showing the planking of Grundy's original construction

Humber Sloop entering the barrel-sided lock at Keddington

The names of the locks, taken from John Padley's survey were:

Tetney Lock
Out Fen Lock
Alvingham Lock
Salter Fen Lock
Willows' Lock
Ticklepenny's Lock
Keddington Church Lock
Top or Louth Lock

He reported the River Head to be 66' 6" wide, with a depth of 6' 5". Padley reported the surface water was 51' 1" higher than the land sill of Tetney lock.

In his original report of 1756 Grundy gave the following information regarding the names of the locks and the fall of water at the sill:

> "...From the upper end of Alvingham Fen to Louth there being a rise of 56' 1", it is proposed to carry up the navigation in 9 locks."

The fall of water at each of the proposed locks was calculated to be:

At the upper end of Alvingham Fen,	of 6' 7"
By Alvingham Mill,	of 6' 2"
In Alvingham Field and a	
Close of Mr. Scrope,	of 6' 5"
At Keddington End,	of 4' 4"
At Keddington Mill,	of 5' 11"
Against Keddington Church,	of 5' 6"
In Mallard Ings,	of 6' 11"
By the side of the Leather Mill,	of 5' 3"
By the side of Mr Thorold's	
Lower Mill,	of 8' 8"

This table shows there to be nine locks, however, add Tetney sea lock and we have a total of 10. In fact only 8 locks, including Tetney lock, were built. The lock by Mr. Thorold's Lower Mill, where the Crown Roller Mills development is in Ramsgate, was not built, neither was the lock by the side of the Leather Mill close to the Riverhead.

TOLLS

The Commissioners had been granted powers under the Act to lease or let the tolls for the best sum they could obtain. Tolls were the only means by which the Commissioners or the lessee could raise money to pay for the canals upkeep and running. They were also necessary to pay the promised 5% per annum interest to the investors.

The Act required that the lease period should not to exceed seven years. On the 20th January 1770 Charles Chaplin, one of the Canal Commissioners, contracted to take the tolls for a period of seven years at the lease rate of 4 per cent per annum payable to the shareholders. In addition to this he agreed to pay all costs and charges, and maintain the navigation to the extent of £500 per annum. He must have thought the income from the tolls, collected from trade on the canal, would warrant his bidding for the tolls. There was one clause in the agreement to the effect that, if his costs were to exceed £500, then the commissioners would pay the excess. Chaplin was also given the right to renew the lease after the seven year period was up. The new rate was to be set at 6 per cent per annum.

The early tolls charged on the Navigation were set as:

All goods and Wares, Merchandise or commodities:

except groceries.................................... 4s per ton
All groceries.. 8s per ton

A minute of the 16th May 1777 stated the tolls were to be let for a seven year period. An advertisement was to be placed in the Cambridge Chronicle and York Courant. The notice read:

Louth Navigation.

"This is to give notice, that the commissioners for the said Navigation do intend to let or lease the Tolls arising thereon, for the term not exceeding seven years, when and where all persons concerned therein are desired to attend by themselves or agents. By order of the Commissioners.
Jolland their Clerk."

This meeting was set for the 12th June. It had been agreed that Chaplin should obtain an engineering report of the condition of the Navigation for this meeting to let the tolls. However, the meeting did not take place on the due date.

By the 24th June, the date when Chaplin's first seven year term should have ended, the Commissioners had requested that he continue with the management of the canal and its tolls until the next meeting.

This took place in the 12th August at the Blue Stone Inn in Louth. Those present were; Charles Chaplin, Lady Chaplin, Lord Scarborough, The Warden of Louth, Mr Nicholas Wrigglesworth for himself, Mr Floyer Esq., Bentley Bennett Esq., Mr Allenby, Henry Andrews Esq., Mr Frederick L'Oste for himself and the Rev. Joseph L'Oste, Mr Lee, Mr Samuel Pettener for himself and his mother, Mrs Sarah Pettener, Mr Nicholas Shaw, Mr Richard Wharfe, Dr. Sibthorpe, The Vicar and church wardens of Louth, Dr. Clarke and Mr Alexander Gunniss.

At the meeting Chaplin suggested he would contract with the Commissioners for a period of 99 years. He proposed to advance all the necessary money for the repair of the navigation. The original work, apparently, had not been done too well. He agreed to keep the navigation in repair, subject to the orders of the Commissioners, pay the officers' salaries and all other expenses and pay 5 per cent per annum interest, paid half yearly to the subscribers.

All the subscribers agreed to this proposal with the exception of Dr. Clarke and Alexander Gunniss.

A further meeting was called for the 15th September when the clerk was to have drawn up the draft agreement. This was then sent to Mr Beatniffe of Hull who was a barrister. He was to set this out formally and return it in time for the next scheduled meeting on 27th October. At that meeting the agreement was read out in full and they agreed to join Mr Chaplin in obtaining an Act of Parliament to verify the agreement. It was further agreed that the tolls should be vested in Mr Chaplin from the 24th June 1777 when his formal agreement had run out.

This agreement, quite obviously, contravened the Act, but was not queried for over 50 years; despite the Commissioners decision not being unanimous. The Chaplin family in fact gained a controlling interest in the canal that became hereditary in clear contravention of the Act of 1763. They were able to do this as they were the dominant landed family close to Louth. They had their landed base at the village of Tathwell. Their control illustrates the political, social and economic dominance of the landed classes at this time

The Chaplins belonged to a wealthy landed clan living in Lincolnshire in the 18th and 19th centuries. They were wealthy and significant enough for their sons to marry daughters of the aristocracy. One, John Thomas Chaplin married Lady Elizabeth Cecil daughter of Brownlow Cecil the 8th Earl of Exeter. The Chaplins were upper gentry with links to the aristocracy. They had four bases of influence and power in Lincolnshire, two of which were Tathwell Hall near Louth and Thorpe Hall, South Elkington, Louth. Directories of the time show them owning many thousands of acres of land.

Nine Commissioners were appointed to enter into the agreement to carry out the order. He also agreed to make repairs up to the sum of £500 per annum thereafter the Commissioners would reimburse.

One practice of which Chaplin was accused was to encourage his employees, to raise the height of the water in the Navigation. By doing this he overcame the problem and expense of clearing the silting up of the canal. This now caused problems of flooding in certain areas along the route and meant that the Navigation lost its ability to drain the surrounding farm lands.

The complaints made against Chaplin resulted in demands that the 1777 agreement be made void. However, unsurprisingly little support could be found and the matter dropped.

In 1782 the Commissioners had to remind Chaplin that he had not been paying interest regularly. As there was no improvement by 1788 he was ordered to attend annually at Louth to make payments.

By 1792 there were complaints that the canal was not being properly maintained. There was considerable silting, and horses had to be used to tow the boats rather than the craft being sailed. To obtain sufficient depth of water it was necessary to raise the water level above the limits which would allow proper drainage of the surrounding land. The consequence of this move was frequent flooding of farm land. The local farmers were not at all happy about the situation.

Although the Commissioners made orders requiring Chaplin to carry out the necessary repair work, he ignored them. Chaplin hardly did any repair or maintenance work. Boatmen continued to make complaints about the bad state of the canal.

One boat owner stated that, when the canal had been operating effectively, it took him only one day to navigate the canal with one horse. Now it took him two days with two horses at considerable cost. The lock keeper at Tetney was dismissed from his post, accused of raising the water levels and hiring out horses for towing barges. He was on to a good thing!

In late August of 1792 the evidence of the Master of the "William and Mary" sloop was taken. He stated that he used to come up the canal in one day drawing 5' of water, now he has difficulty in doing it in two drawing 4' 2" of water. He used to pay 14s 6d for haulage and now has to pay 18s. He reckoned that from Thoresby Bridge to Alvingham Out Fen Lock there was no more than 4' of water in the canal.

From all this evidence it can clearly be seen that Chaplin had neglected the navigation and caused major problems for the boat owners with the knock on effect in the prices of goods to the people of Louth. During this period Chaplin had been collecting the tolls.

After Chaplin's death, his son, Thomas took control of the canal. He had doubts as to his right to the lease, having regard to the Act and its seven year lease clause. He asked for all monies his father had spent on the canal to be refunded to him, Thomas. In return, he would relinquish his right to the remainder of the 99 year lease. The proposition appears to have been accepted, but was not acted upon, for in 1811, when the canal was once again in a poor state, Thomas' son George widened and deepened the canal to the satisfaction of the Commissioners. In 1814 George spent a further £400 on improvements.

We do not know the tolls for this period, but an estimate of £2,000 per annum was collected in the late 1770's. This had risen to around £5,000 in the late 1820's. During this period the interest had remained constant at £1375, i.e. 5 per cent pa. Chaplin maintained that the canal had not been profitable until the late 1820's.

By the 1820s a clear anti-Chaplin faction had emerged amongst the commissioners, led by Stephen Gray, merchant and John Naull , Louth brick and tile maker.

The opposition was coming from the local commercial classes who resented the controlling interest of the local landed family. Traders in the town complained, that they were being unjustifiably exploited by the Chaplin family. They maintained that the tolls, which had been fixed in 1763, needed revising to take into account the increased trade on the navigation.

This commercial opposition was trying to prevent the Chaplins from legalising their position through a new act of parliament. They challenged their lease through the court of chancery, which actually found against the Chaplins. The opposition also lobbied parliament by circulating written objections amongst M.P.s. However they were unable to prevent the passage of a bill in 1828 legalising the Chaplins' control of the lease for the remainder of the 99 year period. George Chaplin of Tathwell and Francis Chaplin of

Riseholme had the tolls for a further 48 years. The tolls were also reduced, thus going some way to meeting the complaints of the traders.

Given their local landed wealth the Chaplin family were in a strong position. Also a number of Commissioners were members of their family, and several others were friendly with them. They could use their own influence as leading landowners and that of others to gain the support of a parliament dominated and run in the interests of the landed classes in the 1820s. A member of the family, a Charles Chaplin, was M.P. for Blankney, Lincolnshire from 1818 – 1831.

At the time of the new Act, in 1828, a survey was carried out by Mr. J. S. Padley. He was asked to survey the whole canal as there were many problems with the depth of water and the condition of the locks. Padley found there was much silting up of the canal and that several of the locks were found to be overhanging at the top by as much as 24". Alvingham lock was in a "bad state". Salter Fen Lock was described as, "getting weak and bad, and will soon be ruinous".

It was quite obvious that major work was required to make sure the canal could continue with trade. Work was put in hand and the necessary repairs carried out. It was often necessary to drain parts of the canal between locks or in some instances the whole canal itself when these works had to be carried out.

The 1828 Act obtained for "maintaining and improving" the navigation and for the alteration of the tolls amounted to 3d or 4d per mile per ton depending on the goods and on every quarter of corn to 1/2d per mile.

The tolls produced for the 1828 Act make interesting reading for they give a clear idea of the type of goods being brought up and down the Navigation. They are:

CANAL TOLLS – 1828

	£	s.	d.
For every ton of sugar, molasses, plums, currants, raisins, and figs, the sum of:	4	0	- 4 per mile
For every ton of slate, timber, deals, and freestone, the Sum of:	2	8	- 3 per mile
For every chaldron of coals of forty-eight bushels - Imperial measurements, the sum of:	2	8	- 3 per mile
For every forty bushels of cinders, coke, or culm – the sum of:	1	4	- 1 per mile
For every eighty Tods of wool of twenty-eight pounds to each Tod, the sum of:	2	8	- 3 per mile

For every one thousand of stock bricks, paving bricks, floor bricks, or pantiles, the sum of:	2	8	- 3 per mile
For every one thousand common bricks, the sum of:	1	4	- 1 per mile
For every quarter of Rye-grass seed and Hay seed, the sum of:	0	2	- ------------
For every four quarters of Rye-grass seed and Hay-seed the sum of:	-	-	- 1 per mile
For every twelve bunches of plaster laths, the sum of:	0	4	- ------------
For every fifteen bunches of plaster laths, the sum of:	-	-	- per mile
Foe every quarter of Wheat, beans, peas, rye, lentils, Barley Malt, Oats, Rape Seed, or Linseed, the sum of:	0	6	- per mile
For every ton of all other goods, wares, merchandize, and commodities whatsoever, the sum of:	2	8	- 3 per mile

And so in proportion for any greater or less weight or quantity of the several articles before enumerated than the Ton or Quantity before-mentioned.

It is interesting to note that the vast majority of good listed above were imports rather than exports. This was a weakness of the trade on the canal from the very early stage and together with the coming of the railway ultimately led to its decline.

One problem that the boat owners faced was the wind direction at Tetney. If an easterly were blowing the vessels could not escape the Haven and so could be tied up for days or even weeks. To help solve this problem Frederick Chaplin had provided a steamer to tow the vessels from White Gate at Tetney Lock and out of the Haven. The Louth Steam Navigation was later formed in the 1880's to solve this very problem.

TRADE

With the arrival of the canal Louth was to derive considerable benefits as trade quickly began to pick up. Barges dealt in large quantities of coal, grain, wool, oil-seed, timber and all kinds of building materials. Tanneries, timber yards, grain warehouses, boat building yards and oil cake mills were but a few of the many businesses which were soon thriving around the Riverhead.

A look at William Brown's panoramic view of Louth in the Council Chamber in the Town Hall, painted around 1846, will give a clear idea of the numerous industries situated there. By this time it clearly lived up to Cragg's description in 1799 of the Riverhead as:

"Looks like a town at a distance."

The Corporation leased land to a James Dunn so he could establish a road with commercial buildings to cope with the new trade flooding into the town. The road is now called "James Street" in his honour. Carpet factories and woollen mills were established there.

In the 1770's the canal's main exports were wool, corn and general agricultural products. Imports consisted mainly of coal, timber and groceries. These cargoes had been off-loaded at Hull onto the Keels and Sloops for the journey to Louth. Other products followed as trade picked up. One cargo of monkey nuts consisted of 70 tons. They were on sale in the town for 2/- per pound (10p). That works out at around £220 per ton so the whole cargo was worth about £15,000. Someone was making a fortune out of canal trade.

In Whites 1828 directory the entry for Louth gives some indication of the canals effect on the trade in the town. There were customs officers, sailmakers, chandlers and mariners. One name among the list of mariners catches the eye; it is that of James Ticklepenny. The Ticklepenny family had farmed at Keddington for a number of years. They became lock keepers and toll collectors and had "Ticklepenny Lock" named after them. It appears that at least one member of the family, James, became a mariner.

Evidence from Whites Directories shows Ramsgate, James Street and the Riverhead areas to be the three main dwelling locations for the mariners living in Louth.

Of the many industries and occupations around the Riverhead there were corn merchants. Among some of the names listed were Chapman, Hardy and Sharpley and Lawrence. William Edwards and Isaac Needham were corn millers too. Needham also had a bone crushing mill.

There were coal merchants, a blacksmith, maltster, ship builders and three timber merchants. The name of William Hardy appears under the list of coal and timber merchants as well as a corn merchant.

The wool agents and staplers were Chapman and Foster. The rope and twine manufactures was William Wray, a relation of Thomas Wray the ship builder.

From this list it can be clearly seen that Louth had began to depend on the canal for it prosperity. Not only for the large number of jobs its coming created but the extra trade generated within the town itself. Goods, hitherto, difficult to obtain because of the poor state of the roads and slow transport were now easily obtained by boat from Hull and London. Charles Lawrence of Riverhead is listed as a grocer in the 1842 directory along with nineteen others.

There were at least eleven mariners recorded in the 1842 Directory, ten of them living in Riverhead, the eleventh living in Victoria Terrace. Other trades and industries having connections with the canal were; Blacksmiths, boat builders, bone crushers, brewers, brickmakers, butchers, coal and corn merchants, corn millers and fishmongers.

There were grocers, inn keepers, beer houses, drapers, maltsters, nail makers, rope makers, seed merchants, timber merchants, wharfingers - three at the Riverhead, wheelwrights, wine and spirit merchants to mention but a few. It is quite clear that a great many people owed their livelihood to the coming of the navigation.

In 1822 vessels were trading from Gray's Wharfe to London and Hull. In 1835 the London, Louth and Yarborough sailed alternately to London about every ten days. The Magnet, Reliance and Resolution sailed alternately, once a week to Hull. By 1841 the Albion, Lough and Yarborough were sailing fortnightly to London from Nell's Wharfe. The Magnet, Reliance and Resolution continued their weekly trips to Hull from the same Wharf.

In 1842 trading vessels left "Nell's" wharf once a fortnight for London. They were the Yarburgh, Britannia and London. Boats left for Grimsby, Hull, Leeds and all parts of the West Riding of Yorkshire on a regular basis from the Riverhead.

A BLOT ON THE HORIZON

The story of the lease does not end at this time, for in 1846 an Act of Parliament was passed. It authorised the establishment of the East Lincolnshire Railway Company (ELR) and for them to construct a railway from Boston to Grimsby and transferred the lease for the canal to them. This would mean Louth would now become part of a national network of railways.

In July of 1847 Miss Charlotte Pye laid the foundation stone for the railway station. In March 1848 a regular train service began to Grimsby. A full service to London did not commence until September of that year. In the meantime the ELR had purchased the Chaplin lease for the Navigation and subsequently the GNR Company took over that lease for the remainder of its life in 1876.

A second Act enabled the Great Northern Railway Company (GNR) to purchase the East Lincolnshire Railway.

So the navigation now became part of the Great Northern Railway Empire for the remaining 29 years of the 99 year lease. The G.N.R., quite obviously, took on the lease to prevent the canal from competing with them. They would, also, have put the toll charges up to the maximum the Act permitted. This would make the transportation of goods considerably more attractive by rail than water.

However, businesses continued to use the Navigation for trading. This can be seen in the income from tolls the Commissioners received after the GNR had relinquished its lease in 1876 for in 1887 they received £1,417, not an insubstantial sum.

THE RIVERHEAD IN ACTION

From its beginning in 1770 the Riverhead developed a unique character as an inland port. This came from the businesses that grew up around the area where the boats loaded and unloaded the goods they took in and out of Louth. At first it was predominantly commercial in character but later became residential as well.

At the start of the 19th century it was almost separate from the older established market town, as noted by John Cragg in 1799. By 1828 the Riverhead was a community providing employment and income for a broad social group who lived there and were engaged in its trades and businesses.

By the end of the century the Riverhead had been absorbed by, and become part of Louth. The no-mans-land between the Riverhead and the town had been filled by the railway and with its arrival ribbon development had taken place on either side. The slow infilling had begun which continued through the life of the canal and well into the twentieth century.

The nature of its trade changed as well. By 1900, although there were businesses concerned with animal feed and fertilisers, and boats still plied to and from the wharves to places such as Hull, Wakefield, Leeds and London, the trade and in particular the employment connected to the canal had shrunk considerably. The arrival of the railway in Louth in 1848, ultimately led to the decline of navigation trade. However, this happened very gradually and certainly did not affect it greatly at the time. It was to be another 20 to 30 years before its closure appeared to be a foregone conclusion.

The streets that grew up in this area around the canal basin were; Riverhead Road, Riverhead Terrace, Thames Street, Commercial Road and Eastfield Road. Ramsgate and Trinity Lane have some links as some people who worked at the Riverhead lived here. However our focus is the immediate area around the inland port.

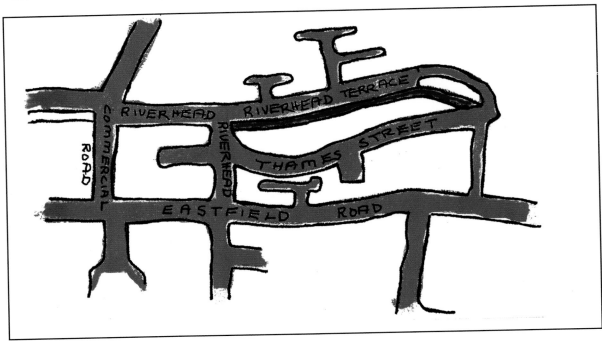

Fig 1. The area around the Riverhead as it is today

By 1805, the enclosure award map for Louth shows that Riverhead Road, Thames Street, and Eastfield Road leading from Eastgate were already laid out. Commercial Road and Riverhead Terrace did not as yet exist. At this early point in the 19th century the impression gained from the enclosure map is of an area that was still largely open countryside divided up into fields. (See Fig 2).

Over time the fields would become plots that were sold off for both commercial and residential use. The description given by a John Cragg, of Sleaford visiting Louth in

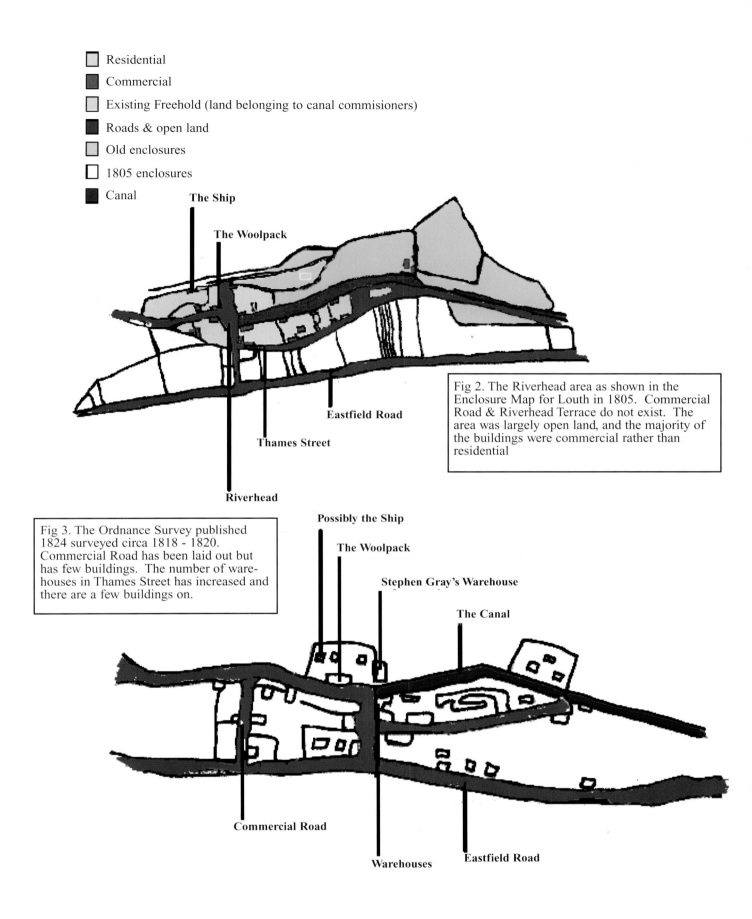

Residential
Commercial
Existing Freehold (land belonging to canal commisioners)
Roads & open land
Old enclosures
1805 enclosures
Canal

The Ship

The Woolpack

Eastfield Road

Thames Street

Riverhead

Fig 2. The Riverhead area as shown in the Enclosure Map for Louth in 1805. Commercial Road & Riverhead Terrace do not exist. The area was largely open land, and the majority of the buildings were commercial rather than residential

Fig 3. The Ordnance Survey published 1824 surveyed circa 1818 - 1820. Commercial Road has been laid out but has few buildings. The number of warehouses in Thames Street has increased and there are a few buildings on.

Possibly the Ship

The Woolpack

Stephen Gray's Warehouse

The Canal

Commercial Road

Warehouses

Eastfield Road

1799 is rather different and may have been exaggerated perhaps to liven up his account or to 'sell' the Riverhead. He said it was separate from Louth 'about half a mile east of the town' and consisted of several wool warehouses and granaries and it looked 'like a town at a distance.'

The 1805 map showed only six buildings classed as residential and about eighteen classed as commercial scattered around the area, which had more open than built up space. The south side of Thames Street was empty, as was the whole of Eastfield Road. The two warehouses that still flank the head of the canal were there at that date. It is also possible to identify the Woolpack Inn which was built around 1772 shortly after the canal opened.

At this time wool was a significant export from Louth but was not so important later on during the 19th century. The Woolpack reflects this original trade in its name and was built to take advantage of the canal and cater to the needs of those involved. The buildings that may have formed the nucleus of the Ship Inn, the other major public house associated with the canal are possibly behind the Woolpack. Pigots Directory of 1822 does list the Ship Inn with a William Cartwright as publican. Most of the buildings in the area are to be found between the south side of the canal and Thames Street. There is little on the north bank.

The Ordnance Survey map dated 1824 gives us some idea of development by 1820 as it was based on a survey carried out between 1818 and 1820. (See Fig 3). Commercial Road now exists but has only two to three properties on it. The buildings between the canal and Thames Street, presumably warehouses have increased and been enlarged. There are now a few buildings along Eastfield Road. The complex of buildings that made up the Woolpack can possibly be identified, but it is not clear if the Ship Inn is marked on the map.

As in 1805, the north bank of the canal has few buildings. In particular the two dry docks that were part of the two shipyards noted by Padley in his survey of 1828 are not marked on the map. However one may have been there by 1822 as Pigot's Directory of that year refers to Thomas Wray, boat builder, Waterside.

In fact a comparison of the OS map of 1824 (Fig 3) with Padley's Survey of 1828 (Fig 4) suggests a quickening of trade and the increasing development of the Riverhead as a functioning economic area between 1820 and 1828. The north bank has more development. In particular there are now two ship builders. One dry dock and associated workshops have been developed by Richard Nell (1772-1828). Padley records this as being in the hands of his executors. This complex includes a blacksmith's and a block maker's shop. It is possible Richard Nell also built the house he lived in behind the shipyard.

A second dry dock is also evident, presumably the one developed by the Wray family. They were already established boat wrights on the River Trent at Alkborough and one branch of the family moved to the Riverhead in Louth presumably they felt it was a good commercial proposition. Their holding was not as extensive as that of Richard Nell as it only included a wood shop in addition to the dry dock. Similarly they lived in a house within the general area of the yard.

Buildings and Yards at Riverhead In 1828

Numbers correspond to those of the map.

1:      Grounds with rope makers shop.

2:      Malt Kiln with granary over the top. Built over the River Lud.

3-5:   Yard and Tow Path.

6:      Bone Mill and Yard.

7:      Gas Works.

8:      Yard with buildings made of stud.

9:      Merchants Yard and Office.

10:     Bain's Water Mill.

11:     Garden.

12:     Merchants Yard. On the north side (canal bank) is part of a granary. The remainder is a drying kiln with a granary over, it has three floors. The buildings to the east comprise of a woodshed with granary over the whole length. Buildings fronting Thames Street comprise two tenements.

13:     Garden with a bridge over the Lud.

14:     Garden.

15:     Building running north/south (canal to Thames Street) comprise of an office with stables and a granary running over the whole length. Under this building is a 4' feeder tunnel from the Lud to the canal. This is used to keep the level in the basin at a constant height. It is only used when Bain's Water Mill is not in use.

16-18: On the street (Thames Street) there is a house; in the grounds is a stable and a piggery. In this plot there was another house, a granary, a bone steam mill, a flour mill with two floors above. A drying kiln to the flour mill and a stable with a granary over the top.

19:     House over the River Lud to the east. To the west is a tenement.

20:     Granary over the River Lud.

21: Warehouse on the canal side at the Riverhead – has a ground floor with two others above.

22: At the junction of the Riverhead and Thames Street there is an office, stable, tenements, shoemakers and a tailors shops.

23-24: Across Riverhead Road is a blacksmiths, a stable with granary over the River Lud. The granary has a ground floor with two floors above. An Office and a house are in the grounds.

25: Five tenements with gardens.

26: Granary built over the River Lud.

27: Fields.

28: Mill.

29: Ship public house with stables and out buildings.

30-32: Farm buildings yard and land.

33: Gardens.

34: Riverhead Road, two tenements, stables and gardens. A yard with stables which are divided into 8.
Woolpack public house with stables, brew house and out buildings.

35: Warehouse at the Riverhead on the canal bank. The rest is a coal yard.

36: Old course of the River Lud before it was diverted to its new course in Thames Street at the time of the canals construction.

37: Several buildings – a granary comprising cellars, ground floor and two others. Tenements and stables.

38: Road.

39: Granary.

40: Garden and a saw shed.

41: Old course of the River Lud.

42: Tenement with garden.

43: Yard and buildings with a granary over the top.

44: Garden.

45: Ship yard comprising; dry dock, blockmaker's shop, blacksmiths along with yards.

46:     House with garden (Richard Nell's).

47:     Old course of the River Lud.

48:     Dry dock, buildings and a wood shed.

49:     House with garden.

William Brown painted the Riverhead in 1844

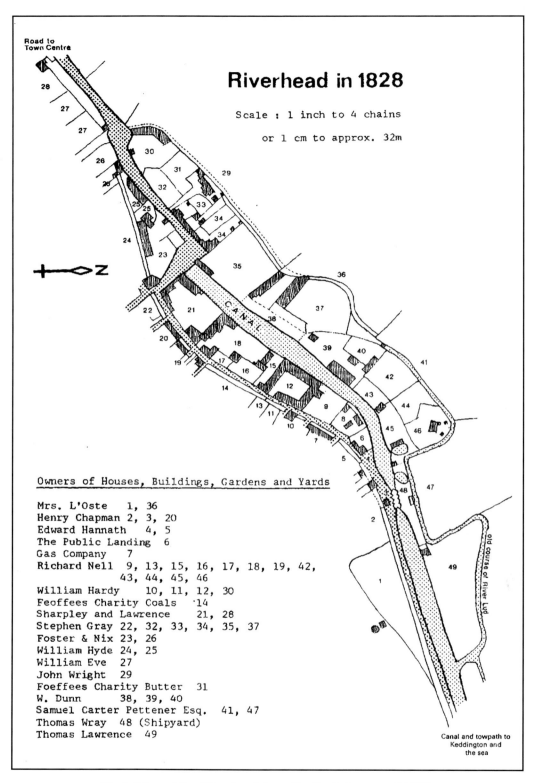

Riverhead in 1828

Scale : 1 inch to 4 chains

or 1 cm to approx. 32m

Road to Town Centre

CANAL

Old course of River Lud

Canal and towpath to Keddington and the sea

Owners of Houses, Buildings, Gardens and Yards

Mrs. L'Oste   1, 36
Henry Chapman 2, 3, 20
Edward Hannath   4, 5
The Public Landing 6
Gas Company   7
Richard Nell 9, 13, 15, 16, 17, 18, 19, 42,
              43, 44, 45, 46
William Hardy   10, 11, 12, 30
Feoffees Charity Coals ·14
Sharpley and Lawrence   21, 28
Stephen Gray 22, 32, 33, 34, 35, 37
Foster & Nix 23, 26
William Hyde 24, 25
William Eve   27
John Wright   29
Foeffees Charity Butter   31
W. Dunn   38, 39, 40
Samuel Carter Pettener Esq.   41, 47
Thomas Wray 48 (Shipyard)
Thomas Lawrence 49

Fig 4. Plan of the Riverhead from Padley's Survey of 1828

Moving in an easterly direction along the north bank Padley shows that there are new blocks of buildings with others situated behind them, just before the bend in the basin. Nothing is shown at this position on the 1824 OS map (surveyed 1818-1820). William Dunn ran this complex, comprising granaries, stables, tenements and a yard. This is the typical integration of commercial and residential buildings for the time.

Further along the north bank, the complex of buildings associated with the Woolpack appears to have been extended and enlarged. It now definitely included a brew house and a number of stables, as well as some tenements. Likewise the Ship Inn appears as a larger block. Further tenements and a farm had been in the area where the swimming pool and the theatre are today.

As well as buildings on both banks of the canal there were merchant's yards near the wharves where goods, primarily coal, corn and timber were loaded and unloaded. The south sides of Riverhead Road and Thames Street have more tenements and granaries. The area which from 1805 had been the most developed, between the canal basin and Thames Street has also expanded. The other part of Richard Nell's commercial empire was situated here. By 1828 this included granaries, a drying kiln, a bone steam mill, a flour mill, stables and offices. Other merchants had similar premises here.

It is clear that between 1805 and 1828 the amount of both commercial and residential buildings had increased. In particular the Riverhead had become much more like the town John Cragg had described it as in 1799. It was now very much a community with tenement blocks to house those employed in the expanding Riverhead businesses. Pigot's Directory for the same year as Padley, 1828, lists 6 merchants who traded in coal and corn. Of these, 4 also traded in timber whilst one other dealt in coal and timber. There were 2 corn millers. The trade in corn and coal remained important until the 1870s. It survived, although to a lesser extent, until after 1900.

From 1841 it is possible to have a much more detailed knowledge of the Riverhead as the census returns now gave details about individuals rather than just an aggregation of the population. From these returns we can get a much clearer picture of the development of the Riverhead and its associated industries and people.

A study of the censuses for 1841, 1851, 1871, and 1891 gives an understanding of its development. Other sources, such as trade directories, lists of toll charges and records of repairs at the Smiths' and Wray's shipyards give additional information. The directories give details about those who ran trades and businesses. The census helps to find out about those who worked in them.

Categories used to analyse the Riverhead and its Population

1. Those directly linked to the navigation --- ship builders, boatwrights, mariners, and sailors.
2. Those whose trade depended on goods transported up and down the canal such as coal, corn and timber.
3. Those whose business began with goods traded on the canal but which could survive apart from it. These were the animal feed and fertiliser businesses.

4. Those whose employment will be described as general services responding to the needs of the inhabitants of the Riverhead, and later on to the town of Louth in general.
5. Those households with servants, the overall number of servants, the number of resident merchants and professionals and those of independent means. This helps in an understanding of the socio-economic nature of the area.

In 1841 the number of households in the area designated as the Riverhead was 76. By 1851 this had increased to 124 with 6 classed as uninhabited. This was probably the greatest amount of expansion at any point in the 19th century. From 1851 to the end of the century the number of households in the area remained stable at 124 to 127. In both 1851 and 1871 6 houses were uninhabited. In 1891 there were 16. This might suggest some decline in employment arising from water borne trade.

The numbers employed in category 1, ship building and as mariners, followed the pattern of increases in households, with the greatest rise occurring 1841-1851. The increase in those employed in shipbuilding was from 16 to 19 and as mariners from 19 to 38. This had dropped to 6 in shipbuilding and 24 as mariners by 1871.

Towards the end of the century in the 1891 census the numbers involved in shipbuilding remained stable at seven, whilst the number of mariners in the Riverhead area was fifteen. This does not include mariners who lived elsewhere in Louth such as Trinity Lane and Ramsgate of which there were another six in 1872 (White's Directory) and three in 1892 (White's Directory).

There was definitely employment for mariners and ship builders, even until 1914. This was not at the peak of 1851 figures three years after the railway came to Louth. However it is clear that water borne trade must have remained as a significant factor at the Riverhead.

An analysis of the records of ships repaired or maintained at the Wray and Smith shipyards 1892 –1914 shows a particular pattern of boat ownership around 1890-1914. The three leading families connected with the Riverhead from at least 1840 were the major owners. Each family between them owned either 4 or 5 boats. Thus the Nells, R.J. and A.M. owned 4 boats, the Smiths had 5 and Norfolk and Sons had 5. Overall from 1892-1900, twenty-three separate owners had boats maintained at the two Riverhead shipyards.

The other owners appear to be master mariners owning and running one boat. There is a J. Turpin owning the Mizpah in 1892 and 1906 who is very likely to be the J. Turpin living at 17 Riverhead Road (1892 White's) and absent, presumably at sea, when the census was taken in 1891. His wife Mary was recorded as still married and as head of the household for census purposes.

Other master mariners similarly owning one boat were A. Brook, M. Aaron, and W Buttery. There is an R. Maltby, whose family also functioned as mariners. All of these owners must have felt that boat ownership was a rewarding way to invest their money, especially those who put money into one boat. Albert Brooke named his boat the Annie Forlander, after his daughter Annie Forlander Brooke.

The housing development immediately to the west of the Head of the basin comprising of two blocks of flats in the style of warehouses has the name Forlander Place. It takes its name from the boat.

This raises the question, what was still being traded up and down the canal to make boat ownership worthwhile? The canal was originally conceived as aiding the transport of corn and wool out of Louth and coals, timber and groceries into the town.

For over a century coal and corn remained the major commodities. This can be seen in the number of granaries on Padley's survey 1828. The censuses of the years studied reveal the history of this trade as well as the trade directories. This is the trade classified above as category 2. The number of coal and corn porters remained stable from 1841 to 1851, between 10 and 11.

The numbers of coal and corn merchants can be tracked from 1822, using Pigot's Directory. In 1822 there were 6 combining both commodities and timber. In 1828 there were 7 merchants in coal, corn and timber. By 1842 (White's Directory), this had increased to 13, remaining roughly stable until 1856 (White's Directory) at 11. Timber merchants functioned separately there being 3 in 1842 and 1 in 1856.

There had been a decline in this trade by 1872 when White's Directory records just 4 corn and coal merchants, 1 coal merchant and 2 corn and seed merchants. The only timber merchant in Louth was in Aswell Lane.

By 1892 the entries in White's Directory show that trade in coal and corn had virtually all re-located to the Railway Station area. There were only 5 corn merchants listed in Louth and only 2 of these possibly at the Riverhead. They were Matthew Jackson living at Lud Cottage and J. W. Barton at the Riverhead Roller Mills. Two more were at the Railway station area in Charles Street and one in the Cornmarket.

Of the coal merchants 5 were at the railway station and 2 at the Riverhead. They were T .E .Smith and Son, and Robert Willyman. Two timber merchants, Joseph Bennett, senior and junior lived in Louth but traded in Grimsby. William Nicholson lived on Eastfield Road but his timber business was located at Louth Park. The decline in coal and corn being traded on the canal is evident in the few people employed as corn and coal porters. There were 3 in the 1871 and 1891 censuses.

The table of tolls for the Navigation of 1887 gives us some idea of what was being traded on the canal towards the end of the century. Coal and corn are mentioned which ties in with the evidence from the directories. There were two other types of business that had been developed in the 1820s by Richard Nell in partnership with a Mr. Overton. They became of greater relative significance as the trade in coal and corn declined. These were the production of animal feed and fertiliser. They fall into category 3 as concerns that used the canal to transport raw materials and products but could function as small scale processing plants independently of it. The numbers involved in these concerns remained fairly stable until the early 20th century. Indeed the fertiliser business at the Riverhead remained long after the end of the canal in 1924.

From 1828 there were always 2 fertiliser concerns (category 3). Fertiliser was produced by crushing bones, also by processing guano and phosphates. Robert Norfolk, whose family continued to be involved with Riverhead trade until the 1900s makes an appearance in 1842 as a bone crusher. R. Norfolk and Son were still bone crushers and manure manufacturers in 1892.

Between 1856 and 1881 William Nell senior and junior had a partnership with Thomas Elkington Smith for the production of fertiliser. After William Nell's business collapse 1881-1882, the Smith family carried on by themselves along with the Norfolk's as the other fertiliser firm. The tolls for 1887 include constituents for the fertiliser, bones, bone ash, guano, vitriol, super phosphates and the product itself, artificial manures.

Robert Norfolk was the only seed crusher at the Riverhead in 1842. It is likely he began this trade which produced animal feed. This was done by crushing seeds such as linseed, cottonseed and rapeseed. The process produced oil and the by-product, oil seed cake, was a rich source of protein for feeding to all types of animals. The oil was used in the 19th century in human food and soap manufacture. The 1887 tolls mention all of the seeds used in this process coming in on the canal. Like fertiliser production, the animal feed industry remained stable at 2 from 1851 - 1892.

The Norfolk family was one of these producers and the other one was Thomas Young in the 1850s, followed by William Nell junior until his business failure in the early 1880s. The oil produced in this process is also referred to in the tolls. Rape oil, linseed oil and cotton oil were presumably taken out of Louth on the canal.

Using the census data to look at the numbers employed in the animal feed and fertiliser production businesses one can track their fortunes and extent from 1841-1891. In 1841 category 3 offered the least employment compared with the trade in coal and corn. The figures include those of all social classes who lived and worked in this trade at the Riverhead. There were the merchants, managers and workers such as the coopers. These specialist workers were an important part of the seed crushing business. They made and repaired the barrels in which the oil from the seeds was stored. Others were classified as oil mill labourers or oil millers.

In 1841 out of a total of 19 employed in categories 2 and 3, only 3 were in animal feed and fertiliser, (16%). The decade 1841-1851 was the era of greatest expansion of the inland port. The overall number of those whose employment was linked to the canal in 1857 (categories 1, 2, and 3) was the highest in the century at 94. By 1851 the total employed in categories 2 and 3 was 36, and of these 12 were in feed/fertilisers (33%). By 1871 the proportions had completely reversed. Out of a total of 41, 32 were employed in feed/fertiliser (78%). By this point the overall numbers connected with canal trade had declined to 78 yet the feed/fertiliser businesses had expanded.

Robert Norfolk who was one of the leading feed/fertiliser producers built substantial terraces for his workers that are still lived in today. In 1871 many oil millers, labourers and coopers lived in Norfolk's Place and Norfolk Lane.

Although the number of those employed in connection with the canal had shrunk to 42 by 1891, out of 20 involved with categories 2 and 3 the greatest amount, 65% was still in feed/fertiliser. The decline in numbers employed in feed/fertiliser is reflected in 1891 in the changing nature of those living in Norfolk's Place. It had become a mariner's enclave. Of the 11 houses in the terrace 6 were lived in by mariners, one by a retired mariner and another one by a mariner's widow. Only one was lived in by a cooper.

The canal was still providing employment for mariners and ship builders until 1914. This was supported by a still functioning trade in animal feed/fertilisers, and the tolls of 1887 show that groceries continued to be important. In addition there was considerable trade in the importation of building materials, especially bricks and tiles from the brick making industry at Barton on Humber. Timber, slate, plaster laths and road building materials came up the canal. Wool was exported but was not the important export it had been in the 18th century.

However there had been a major change in the character of the Riverhead by 1891. Despite the fact that an impressive amount of employment was still connected with the navigation in 1891, nearly 50 years after the arrival of the railway, most of those living there were employed in category 4. These were general services such as butchers, shoemakers (known as cordwainers), blacksmiths, beer houses and inns.

Between 1828 and 1871 there were more people employed in those categories linked to the canal (1, 2 and 3) than in general services. In 1828 those that did exist seem to have been for the benefit of the immediate community – the Riverhead. There were the shoemakers situated in the block of buildings that were part of Sharpley and Lawrence's merchants yard, and Thomas Bramhill's blacksmith's shop on Riverhead Road opposite Thames Street. Other people included in this category are gardeners and grooms.

Until the 1871 census there were more people employed in those trades and businesses connected to the canal than in general services. This tells us that the economic focus of the Riverhead was still largely the canal. General services comprised 29% of those employed in 1841, 23% in 1851, returning to the 1841 level at 28% in 1871.

However the situation had reversed by 1891 when general services were 63% of those employed. Thus by that date the Riverhead had lost its unique identity as an inland port, functioning to some extent separately from the market town of Louth. Norfolk Place remained focused on the canal as a mariners' enclave but the other streets were now dominated by employment other than that connected with the canal.

Commercial Road had changed its character between 1851 and 1891. In 1851 it too had functioned as a mariners' enclave there being 11 mariners in 22 houses as well as a widow Elisabeth Smart who was a sloop owner. This had dropped to 6 mariners by 1871. In 1891 the largest single occupational group was ironically the railway workers. There were 6 of these and had thus replaced the mariners of whom there were only 2. The bulk of the employment was in general services with 14 in this category. Commercial Road was now drawn into the general economy of Louth with joiners, a painter, an iron moulder, a police constable and a coachman.

Riverhead Road had also changed in the same way. In 1871, in category 1 there were 8 mariners and sailors as well as the 4 connected with the 2 shipyards. By 1891 this had decreased to 5 mariners and 2 who can be identified with shipbuilding. There were even fewer in the coal and corn trade: 1 coal merchant, 1 coal leader and 1 retired corn porter and 2 in animal feed. As with Commercial Road and Eastfield Road the bulk of those employed were in general services.

Sloop being towed into Keddington Lock by a horse circa 1890

Two Humber Sloops moored at Ticklepenny's Lock

There was also the maintenance of servants by Francis Major as innkeeper at the Woolpack. Here servants could be more in the nature of employees helping to run a business than part of the gentility required of a middle class household. However one of his 4 servants was classed as a governess. This was certainly a badge of middle class status. The only other people to maintain such a specialist servant as a governess were two undoubtedly prestigious merchants, Robert Norfolk and George Sutton.

There was a drop from 19% to 14% in the number of households maintaining servants by 1851. There were more households with servants (17), but they represented a smaller proportion of the total community as the Riverhead expanded. The actual number of servants had also dropped slightly in ten years from 28 to 25.

A similar pattern to 1841 existed of an economically optimistic area. The wealthier resident merchants maintained between 2 –3 servants. Robert Norfolk now had 3 servants, whilst William Nell continued with 3. Leonard Richard Lee, a wine merchant had 2 servants. Henry Falkner, a solicitor and an established middle class professional living at East Cottage, Commercial Road had 3 servants. Two other merchants, George Armitage and Thomas Young maintained one servant, as did two skilled craftsmen. They were the miller, John Dobson, and Thomas Wray the shipwright.

There was also another example of a sawyer, Amiel Hurst, widower, living in Commercial Road who maintained a housekeeper out of necessity. He had 4 children, the eldest aged 15 was a dressmaker, but beneath her were 3 children from 5-13. The housekeeper herself was a widow of 48. For people like Amiel Hurst the death of a wife meant her place had to be taken by paid domestic help that they may well not have taken on otherwise.

The Woolpack now had just 1 servant. The Ship had 2, one of whom was an ostler, (someone in charge of stabling horses at an inn) who was clearly an employee for the business. The other one was designated as a house servant so she may have had a dual role. The beerhouse on Thames Street employed 1 servant to help in the business.

By 1871 there was a clear drop in the proportion of the Riverhead community maintaining servants. This had sunk to a mere 5% of households (6 out of 126). These employed 9 servants. In the 20 years since 1851, the proportion had dropped from 14%, and from 19% thirty years ago in 1841. The Riverhead was changing its nature as a community. It was no longer so economically vibrant. It was still functioning but was not such a good environment for the skilled craftsman. No skilled craftsmen or mariners maintained one servant by 1871. Mark Smith still maintained one servant, but he was a retired ship's carpenter.

The inns and beerhouses seemed less prosperous too. Both the Woolpack and the Ship were run without paid labour. The publicans used their adult daughters as assistants. William Finney ran the beerhouse in Thames Street with the help of his wife.

The fashions had changed for those merchants who continued to profit from the canal. It was not acceptable for this group to live so close to the source of their wealth. Some of the decline in servant keeping can be attributed to the removal of this group to Eastgate and Trinity terrace where they could live in a more genteel fashion close to others of their social status. The source of their wealth was now at a discreet distance. Thomas Elkington Smith and William Nell both made this move.

Only two functioning merchants were now left at the Riverhead. One was Robert Norfolk, oil miller seed crusher and merchant. He had three servants, including a cook. His house was on Eastfield Road looking away from the canal. This location was also a continuation of Eastgate and so may not have appeared to contemporaries as quite the same location as the Riverhead. William Nicholson, a coal and corn merchant was the other one still living at the Riverhead. However, despite a family of three children he had no domestic help.   George Armitage, the only other merchant was retired, aged 81.

By 1891, the decline in the general wealth of the residents can be seen in the pattern of servant keeping. The proportion of households keeping servants had gone up marginally from 5% to 7% (9 out of 127 households), but the total number of servants was the same at 9. There were three resident merchants, who just kept one servant each.

One of these was William Nicholson, by now a widower aged 69, living with his son. He would seem to fall into the category of those who maintained a servant as much for necessity as a badge of class status. He had not had a servant in 1871 when he had a family. John Norfolk, oil miller, seems to be similar. The son of Robert, he remained unmarried at 51. The other one was Matthew Jackson, corn merchant, living at Lud Cottage on Thames Street. One servant assisted his wife with a family of four children under 8.

Overall, the largest groups were men who kept a servant in the absence of a wife, or because the wife was effectively absent due to advancing years. This was true both of the better off as above, and the workers. A fitter's labourer aged 48, with a daughter aged 8 who had been widowed, had a housekeeper. Samuel Kirk, a gas stoker had a housekeeper and although his marital condition was given as married there is no record of a wife in the census. John Brewer, a widower aged 76, and retired machinist foreman living in Norfolk Place had a servant. William Melbourne, a cow keeper aged 70 and a wife of 64 had one servant. George Brown and his wife, both in their 40s appear to be raising two nephews aged 6 and 3, and had the assistance of a servant.

This is a very different pattern of servant keeping to that in 1841 and 1851. Then there were wealthy and prestigious merchants running middle class families with the aid of a number of servants.   Skilled craftsmen, linked to canal trades, all doing well had also been able to maintain one servant.

A view of the Riverhead in winter ca 1950, showing where the firm of T. E. Smith had its warehouse and in the background the artificial manure business which was sold to Louth Corporation as a refuse depot.

VESSELS

The vessels using the navigation were Humber Keels and Sloops, Billy Boys, which were sea going vessels based on the Keel design, Thames Barges and Fishing Cobbles. Later steam ships were to use the navigation. In general, the Keel boats worked from the north bank of the Humber, and the Sloops from the south bank. Of course, the boats were based on both banks of the Humber, and traded on all the inland navigable rivers and canals. They also sailed to Boston and the Wash ports.

During good weather in the summer months they were known to venture further a field. Originally, the boats were constructed of wood, but later they were built of iron. They were able to carry cargoes of between 60 and 120 ton. However, in general ships on the Louth Navigation carried around 50 to 60 tons of goods.

Billyboys, related to the Keels and Sloops, were fore-and-aft rigged with bulwarks. These vessels could sail the North Sea to Europe with cargos and use the Louth Navigation without the bother of discharging its cargo at Hull into Keels or Sloops.

The vessel 'Industry', owned by Mr W. Nettleton of Hull, who was a hay and straw merchant, was a frequent visitor to Louth. In 1811 he was shipping shingle to Alvingham. On a return journey to the Norfolk coast for another load of shingle, she rammed Biergate swing-bridge, causing damage. After the accident the captain took the vessel out to sea and in an unfavourable wind ran it aground so that it could not be reached for examination. The owners of any vessel that caused damage to the structure of the canal were liable for the costs.

The size of Keels and Sloops varied according to the waters they plied.

In the mid nineteenth century the standard length was 57' 2" with a beam of 14' 8", requiring a depth of 6' 6". Towards the end of the century many owners favoured the Sheffield size which was 61' 6" long by 15' 6" wide, with a depth of 7' to 7' 6" amidships.

Louth had its own size of 72' long by 15' wide. These ships were built in Louth, in the ship yards of Thomas Wray and T. E. Smith and Son. The Louth ships, being around 72' in length, could not navigate the canal system which fed into the Humber, Trent and Ouse.

The Louth boat yards were on the north bank of the Riverhead, close to Top Lock. Records for 1822 indicate only one ship yard owned by Thomas Wray who carried out his business on "Waterside". By 1835 there were two dry docks used for boat building and maintenance. The owners were Thomas Smith and Thomas Wray. However, by the 1924 the dock closest to Top Lock was classified as a Basin.

Sloop being towed into Keddington Lock by a horse circa 1890

Two Humber Sloops moored at Ticklepenny's Lock

SS Luda on the Navigation circa 1900

Sloop with cog boat sailing on the marsh section of the Navigation

At the height of the canal's trade the ship-yards built two craft a year each. However, it has to be said that they normally built one craft a year each. Both Smith and Wray employed five carpenters and two sawyers each. There were no machine saws in those days; everything had to be done by hand. In 1822 there were three families of sawyers listed as living in the Riverhead area. The two firms built three types of vessels, Sloops, Keels and Billy Boys. The timber used in their construction was grown locally.

One of the largest firms to use the canal was that of Robert Norfolk and Son, who manufactured Linseed and Cotton Seed Oilcake for the farmers of the district. The firm owned several of the canal boats for the transportation of linseed and cotton seed to its mill. The heaviest cargo to pass through the canal was by the Sloop "Unity" which conveyed 99 tons of linseed for the company. The sloop completely filled the lockpit and had to be manoeuvred in each lock from Tetney to Louth with great care. After the death of Robert Norfolk the business was transferred to Messrs Sowerby and Co. of Grimsby.

Another local firm with businesses around the Riverhead was the Nell family. In 1807 they had the 'Pomona' with Richard Nell as master and part owner with William Nicholson, both of Kingston-upon-Hull. In 1810 they registered the 'Jobson'. They had several sloops built in Louth. The 'Elizabeth Mary' was built in 1824 and the 'Reliance' in 1826. The 'Emily' was built in 1847 with Richard James Nell as master and part owner with William Wright of Hull.

In 1838 Isaac Smith, founder of the firm of C. G. Smith, advertised that, "as the frost had broken, vessels could now come up the canal and he could supply customers with tea from London". Even when the railway opened, in 1848, Smith continued to get his goods via the canal. In April 1851, he advertised that..."Isaac Smith feels much pleasure in referring his friends to another safe arrival of the Zephyr from London."

In 1856 trading vessels left the Riverhead weekly for Hull and Grimsby, and monthly for London. It is difficult to give an average number of sailings in and out of Louth in any one week. However an average of 20 arrivals and departures may appear to be normal during the summer months. The winter time, of course, caused problems. The canal could freeze up in a severe winter.

Another difficulty was the entry to the Humber from Tetney Haven. The area is famous for its easterly winds in the winter and spring. A local saying 'The winds in Tetney 'ole', spelt a long stay for the master and his mate. Boats often had to wait for up to a week or more for favourable winds before they could sail into the Humber.

The names of some of the ships using the canal during its time were; Active, Amity, Annie Forlander, Ebenezer, Harmony, Lizzie, Neptune, Prince of Wales, Providence, Reliance, Sarah Ann, Sarah, Swallow, Venture, Victoria, Vigilance and Unity. In many instances these names came from the owner's family. If there was a change in ownership quite often the boats name changed too.

From a list of captains in 1892 the following were mariners who sailed regularly on the canal: Cawkwells (six), John Davy, Mark Aaron, Alfred Dobson, William Maltby, John Turpin, William Harvey, Samuel Laythorpe, Brooks (four), William Buttery and John Wilkinson.

There is one story that a Captain Cawkwell, of Louth, took a child on one of his trips. At Tetney the child was lost overboard and drowned. The Captain is reputed to have lost his ticket over the incident.

Keels and Sloops were not the only vessels to sail the navigation. Fishing boats, such as Cobbles, made the daily journey up the navigation, to land their fish for sale at the 'Fish Shambles' in the centre of the town. It is recorded that, in 1790, more fresh fish was landed daily in Louth than in Grimsby.

There were steam ships on the canal. The ss Luda, built in Hull in 1887, arrived from Hull weekly with its cargo. It discharged at Harvey's Wharf which was on the north side of Thames Street. There were also the ss Reliance under captain S. Richmond.

A WALK ROUND THE RIVERHEAD

The Riverhead area, as we have seen, was a hive of activity from dawn to dusk. There would be carts arriving and departing with all manner of goods. The area around the two public houses was the scene of much activity. In the Stamford Mercury of 1859 the following report was filed:

> ..."Numerous complaints respecting wagons, both with and without horses, being left in the streets, in front of the public house near the Riverhead, nine wagons were standing in front of the Ship and Woolpack public houses at the Riverhead, four of the wagons having each four horses attached and not a soul near to look after them"...

No doubt they were quenching their thirst in either the Ship or The Woolpack.

The Woolpack, closest to the Canal, was a busy place, it had a brew house adjoining. There was stabling and housing for farm horses at the rear. These horses had brought corn to the Riverhead and would return with coal, linseed and cotton seed. The inn employed an Ostler to look after the horses but, judging by the previous report, he may have spent just as much time in the Woolpack.

Jackson's Warehouse, south side of Riverhead, now a private residence (see below)

Two examples of Warehousing on the south side of the Riverhead basin backing onto Thames Street

It was ideally sited being but 50 yards from the canal. The other inn, The Ship, stood further back from the road and was just as popular with the wagoners and bargees.

At the corner of Riverhead Road stood a number of granaries, later owned by Theodore West and Co. Ltd. These granaries extended as far back as Eastgate Road. To the west of these granaries, and adjoining Eastgate Road, was a long building which used to be a bonded store when salt was taxed. An advertisement of 1828 titled "Salt" reads:

> "Not withstanding the duty on this article has entirely ceased, it can now be purchased for 50/- per ton."

The first warehouse on the North side of the navigation was part of Stephen Gray's commercial empire in the 1820s (see Padley 1828) and at one time was probably used by the Nell family for the storage of grain for export. Following the repeal of the Corn Laws and the advent of Free Trade it was used for the storage of foreign wheat, which had been transferred at Hull to the Louth sloop 'Active', whose skipper was Captain Turpin, and brought up the navigation to Louth.

It is thought to be one of the oldest warehouses at the Riverhead being built around the time the Navigation was opened. Timbers for its construction would have been brought to Hull from Scandinavia or Russia and transhipped to a sloop and brought up the Navigation to Louth. The growth rings on the timbers are very narrow indicating a short growing season.

The warehouse on the other side of the 'Head' may have been used by the Nell family for a time. This warehouse was also used to store grain. In 1828 it was occupied by Messrs Lawrence and Sharpley. Up to the 1950s it was used by Messer's M. Jackson and Son Ltd. followed by Messrs Seymour and Castle, electrical contractors. Today, 2004, it has been transformed into a single dwelling, retaining a number of original features including its mooring rings on the north wall.

Opposite the 'Head' the old grain store owned by Theodore West and Co. Ltd. has been demolished and a new housing development built. It has been given the name of Forlander Place after the sloop Annie Forlander.

Further to the south a number of warehouses have been demolished whilst others have been converted into flats. The large warehouse with four floors was built around 1818 on the site of a tree nursery. The date has caused some confusion for on the restored brickwork on the eastern gable it has 1881. No doubt the mistake was made when the iron numerals were being replaced after repairs. Towards the end of its life as a grain store it was in the ownership of Theodore West and Co. Ltd.

These two illustrations were photographs taken after Seymour and Castle vacated the premises in 2003. It is interesting to note that most of the original machinery was still intact. The photograph opposite shows the grain shoot. The hoist mechanism for lifting grain on and off boats and storing it in the upper floors of the Warehouse is below.

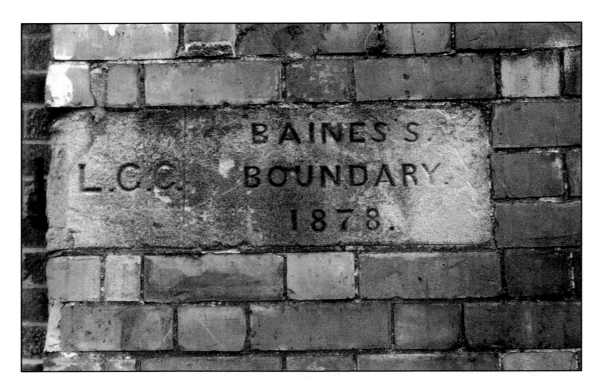

Above shows the boundary line between Baine's Mill and the Louth Gaslight Company whilst the illustration below shows part of the Baine's Mill mechanism

At the west end of Thames Street there was a glove factory, latterly owned by Partridge and Company of Leicester. After the factory was a row of cottages. This was followed by the mill works of Mr R. J. Nell. His mill was used for the manufacture of Linseed and Cotton seed cake, and Linseed oil for the feeding of cattle. The seed was brought to Louth by vessels or horse and cart. The meal consisted of crushed locust beans and monkey nuts.

After the mill closed it was bought and used as a wallpaper-making factory, trading under the name of the Paper Staining Co. On Good Friday, 1905, it caught fire and was destroyed. Opposite was the road leading to Harvey's Wharf. The wharf dealt with general cargoes of paraffin in barrels, groceries, flour, cement and a variety of other goods.

At the entrance to the factory was a courtyard covered in granite and limestone sets. These sets are still there today as a reminder of days gone by. The buildings have rounded corners enabling carts to round the corners without damage to either.

A little further down the road, on the left hand side, stood the Lock Tavern. It is now a private residence.

Beyond the Lock Tavern, on the left, were several buildings including stabling and a piggery, warehouse, granary and a bone steam-mill. This would have caused a terrible stench and not a place to visit. Much of the area once belonged to the Nell family.

Further down, again on the left, stood a large complex of buildings consisting of a merchant's yard containing wool sheds, with granaries over the whole length. There was also a drying kiln with a granary over the top of it and two houses. The complex was, at one time, owned by a Mr Nell and later by M. Jackson and Son Ltd.

On the western boundary of the yard a four-foot brick tunnel had been constructed. It was used to pipe water to the canal basin from the River Lud. When the near-by water mill was not in use the sluice gates could be raised to allow water to flow into the Riverhead to 'top up' the water lost each time a vessel entered or left the basin through Top Lock. These 'feeders', as they were known, were required on all canals if they were not to run dry.

Baines' flourmill stood a little further down on the right hand side. It was built over the river Lud, which flowed down Thames Street, on the south side. The original course of the Lud was to the north and used to flow behind the Ship and Woolpack Inns. It had been diverted when the Riverhead area had been constructed. Grain was brought up the canal or by horse and cart and ground into flour. It was then taken into the town to their bakery in Eastgate to be made into bread and sold in their shop.

Adjoining Peter Baines' corn mill was the Louth Gaslight Company, whose works were erected in 1825. Its main purpose was to provide gas to light and improve the town of Louth. The gasworks were completed in 1826, and the town lit on the 6th April of that year. Lamplighters had to be employed to go round and light each individual gas lamp.

As the Gas works expanded they began to encroach on Baines land. In 1878 he erected a boundary post with an engraved stone recording the exact boundary.

The Gasworks were conveniently sited close to the canal side for the unloading of coal brought by the barges. You can imagine the hustle and bustle of the workmen when a barge arrived.

Originally the coal was barrowed across to the works or piled on the wharf-side, which led to pilfering at nighttime. If the thief's were caught it meant a spell in the House of Correction in the Town.

To avoid this, the Gas Company built a Coal Store with a door on the canal side and another to Thames Street allowing the coal to be stored safely. It could then be barrowed across the road and into the Gasworks.

On the site of the UK coking plant (constructed in 1947/8, adjoining the Gasworks) was the old oil and cake mill, which had started life as a bone mill.

The warehouses opposite were reconstructed in 1909 to provide accommodation for a printing works. The works were owned by Norman Davy Printing Company Ltd. for the printing of high class stationary etc. The business later moved to London. After the First World War the premises were once again occupied, this time by Messrs Billsons and later as Allen Bastrick and Billson Ltd. of Leicester as a glove factory.

In the latter half of the twentieth century the building became a restaurant, however in the early 1970's a fire broke out in the upper floor. There was considerable damage to the top section and roof, so much so that this had to be demolished. Today it is a two-storey building and not it's original three and has been converted into flats.

Further along was a granary, with malt kiln and then a rope makers shop. There were quite a number of houses for the workmen who loaded and unloaded barges or worked in the numerous businesses scattered around the area. Luda Terrace is one such row that was built to house the canal workers.

At this point the Riverhead comes to an end and the final lock on the canal, Top Lock, was to be found. It was quite a dangerous place as there are several recorded deaths by drowning. It was a short cut for people on their way to the businesses on the north bank and to some a way to the Woolpack. One elderly gentleman had gone for his paper and called in at the public house. He spent rather a long time drinking and took a short cut home via the lock. Unfortunately he slipped in and was discovered, the next day, drowned. In another case an old lady slipped on the lock gates as she crossed the lock. She fell in and drowned.

Up a little lane on the right was the Victorian Lock Keepers cottage. Sadly this has been demolished. Just beyond where the Lock Keepers Cottage stood is a row of cottages called Norfolk Place. The cottages had outside loos. They were built by Robert Norfolk for his workers.

The lane led to Eastfield Road. To the left was a steam and windmill belonging to William Griffin. It was destroyed by fire in 1857. The wind got up and caused the machinery to over heat and so the mill caught fire.

To the right about 50 yards towards Louth was the grand house built by Robert Norfolk. Today it is owned by Douglas Electronics.

Crossing over the lock to the north bank would have lead the traveller to the two ship yards of Wray and Smith with their "wet" and "dry" docks. Smith's yard was once owned by the Nell family.

After the ship yards there were many warehouses for the storage of grain. A little further on the wharf side was a 5-ton crane. It was there to aid the loading and off-loading of various cargoes. The wharf side would often be cluttered with resin-pitch and caustic soda, for use in the shipyard and in the town. At the back of Riverhead Cottages was Leather Mill Lane. Another name given to it was Eelmire Road.

For an explanation of 'Leather Mill Lane' we must go back to 1801 and a claim for:

> ..."Allotting and enclosing the open fields, meadows, pasture and other commonable lands and waste grounds in the Parish of Louth." Ann Hubbard, a widow, claimed an ancient stream of water, formerly running through her Estate near the Riverhead."

On that land stood a Leather Mill known as 'Dog Mill'. In the middle of the last century it was a bone-crushing mill. The workers employed there were of Irish descent. It is said that local men would not work there because of the terrible smell. These works were also called "Ich-a-boe". The name came from a small island off the southeast coast of Africa called Ich-a-boe. The fertiliser imported from there was said to be 7.5% stronger than the Peruvian variety.

The Louth Corporation bought the works and converted them into a refuse depot and incinerator. It was used until the 29th September 1954 when the works were sold by auction.

It was not just the Riverhead area that did all the business. All along the canal, from Tetney to Alvingham, wharves had been constructed and warehouses built to take the trade, which was to come up and down the navigation. At Austin Fen in 1856 Mr Motley privately built a warehouse. This was used as a distribution centre, to the surrounding area for groceries, sugar, flour, dried fruit and various other commodities brought up, by barge, from Hull.

At Tetney Lock several warehouses and a lock keepers cottage had been built. It should be remembered that Tetney already had a small port before the coming of the Navigation. Grundy simply used their port as the site for his lock and sluice.

The wharf at Tetney Lock would be a busy place with all the comings and goings of not only boats with goods for Tetney but also the other wharfs along the canal. The inn would be a favourite stopping off place for many a bargee particularly if the wind was in Tetney 'ole or the tide out. A local shop was converted into an Inn and named The Sloop during the late nineteenth century. A name the house retains to this day.

Thoresby Bridge had its warehouse for the storage of grain and other goods. It would serve the villages of North Thoresby, North Coates and Marsh Chapel. It is here that a good example of the land drainage proposed by Grundy in 1756 can be found. On the inland side of the canal can be seen two sluices for the drainage of the waters from the surrounding farm lands.

At Fire Beacon the visitor can still see part of a low warehouse on the east bank of the canal. This is but a small part of a much larger complex of buildings which stood on the west bank, now demolished, for the storage of corn and other goods. The size of the complex can be ascertained from Padley's report of 1828. It also had an Inn, The Ship and was used by the people of Fulstow as their wharf.

At Austin Fen a warehouse had been built in the middle of the nineteenth century. Next to it stood the public house, The Bridge. The wharf was used by the villages of Yarburgh and Grainthorpe.

Alvingham, too, had its wharves. The first was at High Bridge and was used by the people of Ludney and Conisholme for the loading and unloading of goods. The second wharf was at Alvingham Bridge on Lock Road. The road bridge stands to the west of the lock and was, like the majority of others, a swing bridge.

THE RIVERHEAD AND THE NELLS

A name that keeps occurring through-out the life of the Louth Navigation is that of the Nell family. For over nearly 200 hundred years the Nells contributed to the development of trade and shipping in three East coast ports. Those of Grimsby, Hull and Louth were to benefit from their experience. They were importers and exporters as well as mariners, ship builders and owners.

On the solid foundations of the wealth gained through trade they were able to build political careers on local town councils. This meant they had some influence over decision making in the places where they lived and made their wealth.

The first member of the family to trade at the Riverhead in Louth was Richard Nell. However the pattern of commercial activity for the family had already been set in Grimsby and Hull by previous Nells. The Louth family would continue, for about another century, the tradition of port linked trade and activities.

Richard Nell, the Elder, (1714-1796) began the trades that became the hallmark of the family in Grimsby. He was listed in the General Directory of England in 1791 as a corn factor or trader, and coal and raft merchant. The last activity would be connected with trade in wood and planks from places such as the Baltic.

Like later Nells he built up a trade exporting the goods from the surrounding farmland, and importing goods like coal and wood. Using his wealth he was able to buy a position as a Freeman of Grimsby. Given the particular organisation of Grimsby's local government at the time this meant he was eligible to be a member of the town council. He was elected mayor of Grimsby six times between 1755 and 1785. In addition he held a number of important positions in the town such as coroner, magistrate, alderman and bailiff. His son, also Richard, continued the commercial and political successes of the family in Grimsby. He too was a merchant and a mariner and served as mayor seven times 1773-1794.

Another son Thomas (1747-1784) was sent to Louth in 1761 to learn about commerce by being apprenticed to Frederick L'Oste a grocer and chandler. L'Oste was connected with the proposed Louth Navigation and Thomas, no doubt, took a keen interest in this new and potentially profitable project. It may be that Richard Nell the Elder had useful links in Louth and was aware of possible future commercial opportunities there. Potential investors, such as the Duke of Ancaster, were already seriously taking steps to build a canal between Louth and Tetney.

By 1777 Frederick L'Oste was a commissioner for the canal. Certainly to be in Louth in the 1770s was to be in the right place at the right time. Thomas's son Richard (1772-1828), grandson of the Grimsby founder of the dynasty would repeat in Louth the port linked trading activities of his grandfather and uncle in Grimsby.

Before Richard committed himself to a commercial career in Louth he went to live in Hull where he gained invaluable experience, as well as a wife, Elizabeth Hargrave. He is listed in the Hull trade directories 1803-1814 as a Master Mariner and dealer in marine stores. Whilst in Hull he was listed as Master and part owner of the Pomona in 1807 and the Jobson in 1810.

He and Elizabeth returned to Louth in 1814 to the property they already owned at the Riverhead. He brought with him nearly a century of family experience and knowledge of professional and commercial activities connected with the port trade. He and his descendants would go on to have the same sort of influence in local life in Louth as their ancestors had had in Grimsby. The Riverhead had functioned as an inland port for the past forty odd years and Richard clearly felt it to be a suitable place to set up a commercial empire.

Richard Nell developed a broad range of business interests at the Riverhead that seems to have been particularly characteristic of Louth commerce in the 19th century. This involved merchants and those processing raw materials joining together in various partnerships. So it was that one merchant could have a stake in many different shared concerns as well as those he ran solely in his own name.

Richard went into partnership with Thomas Overton as corn, coal and timber merchants, leasing wharves for the loading and unloading of these goods. They also ran a steam mill for milling corn. A survey carried out by James Padley in 1828 reported that Richard Nell had an office, stables, granaries, a bone steam mill, a flour mill a drying kiln and a shades south of the canal on Thames Street. The last building was for the sale of beer and spirits.

Both Nell and Overton joined up with two others, Chapman and Lawrence to set up as bone merchants and bone crushers.

In their time in Louth the Nells mirrored the activities they had carried out in Grimsby and Hull to meet the needs of the surrounding landowners and farmers. To be successful as Louth entrepreneurs they would have to capitalise on this market for fertilisers. Thus the bone trade and bone crushing would cater to the needs of the local farmers. Much of the trade of the Riverhead was linked to Louth's function as a market town for the agricultural hinterland.

Richard ran a ship building business in his own right. He leased land on the north of the canal where he ran one of two shipyards. Given the evidence suggested by a comparison of the 1824 OS map and Padley's Survey of 1828 (see the section on the growth and decline of the Riverhead), it would seem that it was Richard Nell who was responsible for building and developing one of the two ship yards there. As such he made a major contribution to the economy and employment of the area during the 19th century.

There is no reference to a Nell ship building yard in Pigots Directory 1822. His operations later included a dry dock and two workshops, one a blockmaker's and the other a blacksmith's. He rented these out to individual craftsmen. He built the "Elizabeth Mary" here and was part owner of the Sarah, Reliance, Monarch, Emily, Harlequin, Prince of Wales and Jenny. Richard ran a weekly service by boat to Hull in partnership with a Mr. Tummons of Hull and one to London.

Richard, his wife Elizabeth and their large family lived in a comfortable house surrounded by a large garden just behind their shipyard. Again this does not appear on the 1824 OS map so it would seem he built this as well. It was a normal situation for merchants and business men to live close to their enterprises in towns that predated the large industrial factory towns of the mid 19th century. Louth, however, never became such a town.

On the south bank was a tenement of four terraced houses owned and rented out by Richard. These were at the western end of Thames Street. The 1841 census shows that the tenants included three mariners and one agricultural labourer. This was very much in keeping with the nature of the Riverhead as a community with a broad cross section of society at that time.

Richard died in 1828 aged 56, the year in which Padley presented his report on the Canal to the Commissioners. He was by then a Canal Commissioner, a position that he would have hoped would have given him some influence over the running of the canal and the Riverhead. His widow Elizabeth then 46, took over the running of the businesses until son William who was only 16 was able to do so. She did this in a very different way to her husband. She seems to have ended all the business partnerships favoured by her husband.

Whites Directory of Kingston upon Hull and Ports Connected for 1831, lists her alone as a corn, coal and timber merchant as well as wharfinger and the owner of two trading vessels. In a business card she published in July 1830, Elizabeth made it very clear she had ended her partnership with a Mr. Tummon of Hull. She would in future run the weekly service between Louth and Hull alone.

Elizabeth was successful in keeping the range of enterprises going. In Pigots Directory of 1835 William Nell is shown as having taken over the running of the businesses, like his mother, in his own name. William was a coal, corn, bone and timber merchant and wharfinger. Thomas Overton had had to turn to Mr. Newman for a partner in the bone crushing trade at the Riverhead. William carried on the weekly shipping link to London and Hull in his sole name.

William carried on in the same way of business as his mother trading at first in his own name. It is not possible to say what influence Elizabeth had over her son but it is certain that it was not until after she died in 1843 that he reverted to the trading in partnerships like his father. After Richard Nell there is no evidence that the shipyard was run by the family.

The Smith family who were to have a long commercial partnership with the Nells was listed in Pigots directory 1828-29 as beginning their connection with the former Nell shipyard. Mark Smith was running one shipyard and Thomas Wray the other. In the same Directory for 1835 Thomas Wray still runs one and a Thomas Smith, older brother of Mark the other. The census of 1841 lists George Sleight as a shipwright and Whites Directory 1842 names him as running one of the two shipyards and Thomas and Samuel Wray as the other boat builders. By 1856 (White's Directory) Mark Smith is once more listed as running the other shipyard to the Wray's.

William first entered into partnership with his younger brother Richard James. The Nell brothers were described in various directories as trading in the established goods, corn and coal. They had added guano, an imported fertilizer to their list and the production of cake for cattle feed. Whilst continuing port linked activities as wharfingers, ship builders, ship brokers and commercial agents the Nells were expanding those linked directly to agriculture.

Their shipping services to London, Hull, Wakefield and Leeds were advertised as sailing weekly from Nell's wharf in 1846 by Kelly's directory. By 1856 the Nells had gone into partnership with a Mr. Smith adding to their imported fertilizer, guano, with those they were producing themselves such as British guano, and sulphate of ammonia and lime. This was a new step, moving from a business focused mainly on import-export to include the production and processing of goods.

William continued to live in the family home behind the shipyard. The 1841 census reveals a comfortable and wealthy middle class household. There were three servants one male and two female to care for himself, his wife Maria and their young son Richard aged four. An excellent impression of this successful middle class household can be seen in the family portrait painted around 1844. They were still living at the Riverhead at number 53 in the 1851 census. This was the first to give house numbers so we assume it was the house they had always occupied. However by 1861 William and Maria had moved to 179 Eastgate. This area of Louth became the home of many members of the family. It was at a discreet distance from the source of their wealth and trade. The houses they moved to more clearly implied social standing than one behind the shipyard. They were in a terrace known as Trinity Terrace – a fashionable Regency style row of houses which gave them the social standing of living alongside others with local wealth and status. At various times numbers 161, 163, 177, and 179 were owned by Nells. It formed a residential enclave for the family, as well as another Riverhead merchant, Thomas Elkington Smith, who had a significant partnership with two generations of Nells. T .E. Smith lived at 183 Trinity Terrace, Eastgate.

A family portrait painted around 1845 showing William Nell (1812 - 1864) & his wife Mary Martin (1810 - 1892) with their two eldest children, Richard (1837.-.1871) & William (1843 -.1909). The older woman is Mary Martin's mother. The painting is interesting for showing a mercantile family displaying their achieved wealth and status in the manner of gentry.

William Nell 1843 - 1909 with his wife Ann Stephenson and two of his children outside Eastfield House, his new gentry residence, at the height of his social and commercial success, circa 1880

Richard James Nell (1816 - 1868) & his wife Marie Louise McGuffie

Their son Richard James Nell (1849 - 1922) Successful businessman & Mayor of Louth 1888

William Nell died December 14th 1864. An article in the Louth Advertiser 31 December announced that the firm of Nell and Smith would continue trading as before under the eldest son, Richard who was trustee under his father's will. He however died aged 34 seven years later in 1871. The partnership between Nells and Smith went forward with William Nell (1843-1909) the second son of William senior (1812-1864). The Nell and Smith partnership specialised in the production of animal feed, fertilizers (being bone crushers, manure manufacturers, as well as guano merchants). By this time they had moved beyond direct port linked activities.

They continued as ship owners, corn and coal merchants. William Nell junior also ran businesses in his own name as a ship owner, seed crusher and oil cake manufacturer and merchant. All these businesses were carried on at the Riverhead. This shows the Riverhead continuing into the second half of the 19th century as an economically active and productive area even after the arrival of the railway in 1848. William Nell seemed to have reached a pinnacle of commercial and social success by the 1881 census. A list of canal commissioners shows that he became one in 1871. Brother James, described as a merchant in White's directory 1872 also became a commissioner at the same time as, did their partner T. E. Smith.

Sometime before the census of 1881, most likely around 1879 William and wife Alice had moved from 181 Eastgate to a large house they had had built called Eastfield House, currently the Social Services centre. It is large, grand house which stood in extensive grounds. It was situated, at that time, more in the country and gave the owners the appearance of gentry status which is presumably what William wanted. Interestingly, however, it was also but a short walk for William from his grand residence to his business concerns at the Riverhead. He had had two doors built into south wall of the factory for easy access.

Commercial and social success catastrophically collapsed for William sometime between 1881 and 1882. Nell family sources indicate that by the end of 1882 he had lost all his businesses. Certainly he was disqualified as a canal commissioner on April 21 1881, and had been appointed relieving officer and collector to the Louth Board of Guardians by the end of 1882. This was referred to in his obituary notice in the Louth Advertiser February 1909. There is a certain irony in this as it was the equivalent of administering and distributing social security benefits.

William Nell had moved from managing and owning family business interests going back to his grandfather in Louth and living in a prestigious house to being a paid employee of the state. He was forced to move from Eastfield House to a very much more modest property at 9 Sydenham Terrace on Newmarket. The reasons for this complete reversal of fortune are not clear. It has been suggested that it reflected the declining trade linked to water transport given the arrival of the railway. However this had happened over 30 years earlier in Louth and his erstwhile partner T.E. Smith continued to trade apparently profitably at the Riverhead and also by 1900 at the railway station. It is quite possible he had overstretched his business activities, which added to the cost of building Eastfield House caused his collapse. We may, however, never know.

The firm of T. E. Smith, which by 1896 included a son, had taken over those commercial concerns that had for so long been connected with the Nell family at the Riverhead. Kelly's directory for that year referred to the firm as artificial manure manufacturers, coal merchants and ship builders. In 1900 they continued to trade in these concerns at the Riverhead but had also set up as coal merchants at the railway station. Bennet's Business Directory for 1908 and 1911 lists T. E. Smith and Son as bone crushers, another line in which William Nell had been involved. The Smith family continued in business as ship builders and ship owners until at least 1914. They were registered as owning 6 boats between 1892 and 1914.

Although William Nell was a wharfinger and ship owner running trading vessels to both Hull and London weekly he is not listed in directories as a ship builder. Whereas by 1871, if not earlier, a brother of T. E. Smith, George was listed as a ship builder at the Riverhead. He was the younger brother of Mark, the previous owner. The entry also occurs in the 1881 census. The two shipyards would remain with the Smith and Wray families until the end of the century.

Another line of descent from Richard Nell (1772- 1828), that from a son junior to William, Richard James (1816- 1868) survived more successfully commercially. This branch of the family seemed more willing to look further afield. Richard James senior continued the family tradition of mariner with his involvement in the tea and opium trade with China and India between 1840 and 1847. He was the largest shareholder, and a captain on the Torrington, an advanced clipper, the first of British design, built specifically for the China trade.

He married a woman of French and Scottish descent in 1847, Maria Louisa McGuffie. Her father was in business in Haiti and family sources suggest that Maria may have been sent to be educated in London. It is not known where she and Richard James met. It may have been in London as they were married 16th December 1847 in Middlesex. He returned to Louth shortly after his marriage and became involved in the family businesses at the Riverhead. In the 1861 Post Office directory he is a partner in the firm of Nell, Nell and Graves. They were seedcrushers and manufacturers of linseed rape and cotton cakes. There was also an oil mill in Thames Street. At the same time William Nell the older brother was in partnership with T. E. Smith.

Richard James senior had begun an independent role as agent for the Imperial Fire and Life Insurance Office. This would be something his son also Richard James would continue to do. By the 1860s this branch of the family had followed changing transport patterns and re-located the centre of their commercial operations to the vicinity of the railway station.

By 1868 R. J. Nell is listed in the Post Office directory as running the Great Northern oil and cake mill in Charles Street. His Fire and Life Offices were here as well. He had achieved the same pre-eminence in local town politics as the 18th century Nells in Grimsby. He was a town councilor in 1847, 1863 and 1864. Like his older brother William he too died quite young in 1868 at the same age, 52.

The tradition of the Nell family to be involved in local town politics begun in Grimsby in the previous century was further continued in the line descended from Richard James (1816-1868) as his eldest son another Richard James was a town councilor 1876-1885, and in1896 and 1909. He achieved the position of mayor of Louth in 1888. Richard James junior became canal commissioner in 1866, five years before his cousins. William Nell, despite the grandeur of the house he had built on Eastfield Road did not achieve the prominence in local politics symbolized by gaining the position of Mayor as did his cousin Richard James.

The business concerns of this branch of the family were managed by the eldest son, Richard James who was only 19 at the time of his father's death. He was trustee for the family, and in particular for two younger brothers aged 7(Archibald McGuffie) and 12 (George Frederick). He was listed in White's 1872 Directory as the manager of the Great Northern oil and cake mills located in Charles Street. In later directories up to 1896 he is listed as running a seed crushing business and as an animal feed manufacturer and merchant at Charles Street. Presumably this was at the Great Northern Mills. This branch of the Nell family re-located the focus of their operations to the railway station, thus using the new form of transport rather than the waterways network.

In effect they kept a foot in both camps as it were. Between them Archibald and Richard James junior had 3 and possibly 4 boats registered in their names 1892-1899, (Annie/ Reliance, Providence and Ebenezer.) A statement of accounts for 1911 for R. J. Nell and Co. Ltd. cake spice and drug merchants shows that this firm was incorporated in 1897. It is probably at this time that R. J. Nell transferred this operation back to the original centre of Nell family businesses at the Riverhead as that is where the document referred to the office.

Archibald McGuffie Nell was a director along with Martin and Robert Chatterton. Richard James junior was advertising his limited company as merchants and dealers in a variety of animal feed stuffs in the Louth and North Lincolnshire Advertiser May 18th 1898 and based at the Riverhead. They dealt in linseed cakes 'Nell's 95%', cotton cakes 'Nell's Pure', artificial food for young stock, compound lamb food, and Louth calf meal (a milk substitute) as well as Nell's horse spice. In addition brother Archibald remained on his own account in the railway station area as a coal merchant and sheep dip agent.

Between 1887 and 1916 the receipts for the canal show an inexorable decline. The balance of activities at the Riverhead by the end of the 19th century was moving more towards small scale manufacturing and trading concerns connected with agricultural products and away from concerns directly linked to the navigation and port based businesses.

The bulk of business at the Riverhead was now in small scale agro-chemicals and chemicals. William Nell and T. E. Smith were involved in the manufacture of artificial manure 1876-1882, their factory being on the north bank of the canal. T. E. Smith and Son appear as artificial manure manufacturers in Kelly's Directory between 1896 and 1919.The Riverhead did not come to an end as a small scale manufacturing location after the canal itself ceased functioning.

The flood of 1920 ended port based activities and water borne trade and traffic there. T. E. Smith and Son were still functioning there as artificial manure manufacturers in Kelly's Directory of 1926. T. E. Smith & Son were listed as coal merchants at the Riverhead in 1919 (Kelly's Directory) and at the railway station. Other members of the Smith family continued to manufacture at the Riverhead until at least 1945. This is the latest date for which we have an annual account sheet for the firm of Mark Smith Limited, manufacturing chemists, at the Riverhead, which was incorporated in 1893. Earlier in the 1881 census Mark Smith was referred to as a chemist living at

6 Gospelgate. It is not known if his business premises were already at the Riverhead then. He was a son of Thomas Elkington Smith.

It is clear that the Nells had lost their place as the dominant Riverhead commercial dynasty. From the 1880s the Smiths took on this role. William Henry Smith, a younger brother of Mark the chemist was collector of tolls for the Navigation from at least 1905 (the earliest directory reference) until the canal ceased functioning in 1920. He was also a director on the board of his brother's business manufacturing chemicals. Over two hundred years the Riverhead changed its function, but its later role as a location for small-scale manufacturing would never have come about without its origins as an inland port.

Thirsty Work - The Public Houses and Inns along the Louth Canal - 1770-1920

The canal created a corridor of economic opportunity along its length. Trade in beer and other goods appeared, increased and decreased as the canal grew, prospered and ultimately declined. The public houses and beer houses connected with the canal were of different types. There were those that were built specifically as public houses and others where the retailing of beer was a second or even third string after other economic activities. However the retailing of beer can function as a good barometer of the overall economic state of the canal.

An interesting feature of the role of licensed victualler is that it was not a totally male occupation during the 19th century. This was at a time when contemporary and especially middle class culture believed that the role of women was to support the work of men by not joining in employment themselves. The public house however retained the characteristic of an earlier world of work prior to factories when most employment was based in the home. Even where the licensee was a man he would benefit from the labour of his wife and frequently daughters in the business.

The Ship and Woolpack were at the Riverhead inland port where the canal terminated. They were built as public houses to support the trade connected with the import and export of goods via the canal. They were near to clusters of warehouses where goods were stored before further processing, sale or shipment. They provided hospitality for those involved in the business of the canal. They were venues where business deals could be discussed and transacted. They also provided stabling, which was an important service for all trade and transport at this time. The Woolpack had a considerable number of stables.

Along the length of the canal were other public houses. However these often tended not to function solely as beer retail outlets. Such public houses evolved where individuals, usually existing farmers and landowners, saw a number of opportunities for making money from the canal. There has proved to be a very close relationship between farming and victualling along the canal. The sale of alcohol was used as an opportunity for making more income. There were places along the canal where roads and bridges crossed it. Trading points grew up here, again often with warehouses.

Thus at Alvingham where there was a lock as well as a road and bridge wharves were built. Robert Lucas, the adjacent farmer also realised he could profit from the sale of alcohol and coal. At Fire Beacon where a bridge crossed the canal an inn developed near warehouses. Here beer retailing was carried out alongside coal and corn trading and farming.

The Crown and Anchor was at Tetney Lock just before the exit/entrance into the North Sea. It is not possible as yet to say definitely when the Crown and Anchor was built. It is possible it pre-dated the canal. Tetney Lock was an important point on the canal. It was where the canal began and the sea-water was excluded by the sea-lock. Boats had to wait here for the right wind and tide. It was also an administrative point where tolls were charged and there was a toll-collector's cottage. There would be trading on the wharves. There would have been plenty of custom for an entrepreneurial publican. The Crown and Anchor was a cross between the sort of dedicated public house that supported canal trade like the Ship and Woolpack and the opportunistic venues selling beer along the canal corridor. For much of the late 18th and 19th centuries its owners derived a large part of their income from farming.

The Riverhead Public Houses and Beer Houses

The Woolpack

The Riverhead had two public houses and a varying number of beer houses during the 19th century. The public house that was definitely established the earliest was the Woolpack. This was built shortly after the opening of the canal in 1770. It was a response to commercial opportunities at the inland port for refreshment, hospitality and stabling. It was the closest to the canal and its wharves and warehouses. The facilities included a brew-house, stabling and housing for farm horses. The horses brought corn to the Riverhead as well as wool and would take away coal, cotton seed, linseed and groceries.

Stephen Gray, general merchant and wool merchant is the first known owner who bought it in 1813. The symbol above the doorway still today is a wool pack with S.G. on it being Stephen Gray's initials. He owned some land outright at the Riverhead. His other holdings were leased from the commissioners. It was on these that he built up his commercial empire adjacent to the canal. Padley's survey 1828 clearly described this. It included the wharf and warehouse occupied by the LNT today as well as a coal yard. To the right and facing the canal was Gray's other leasehold property, including the Woolpack and its stables. There were additional enclosures, containing yards, tenements, stables and buildings like sheds and outhouses. He also seems from Padley to have leased Occupation Road, which was the access to the Ship Inn.

Gray kept the Woolpack from 1813-1822. Its running was taken over by a Stephen Hancock from 1822-1825. Stephen Gray is described as owner of the Woolpack at the pub today. But the exact status of those who ran it after him is not known. Certainly from Stephen Hancock's time the Woolpack was no longer part of a broad commercial empire in the same way as under Stephen Gray. Gray himself died in 1840, and left his properties and commercial premises to his nephews. Some of these at least, were sold on again by them in 1843.

Francis Willows Mager was the publican for 21 years from 1825-1846. The 1841 census shows him running a very successful business and a household with 6 children, 3 servants and a governess. No other publican ran the business in such style. By this time the separation between the public house and the sort of commercial empire that Stephen

Gray had run was permanent. Mager was succeeded briefly 1846-1851 by William Day. Thereafter the Woolpack was associated for nearly half a century with the family of Richard and Elizabeth Clarke (1851-1892). This was achieved by the tenacity and good health of Elizabeth who took over the running of the pub as licensed victualler on the death of Richard aged 43 in 1855. She ran it on her own for five years until she remarried a William Hewson in 1860. He survived for 7 years at which point widow Hewson took over again 1867 until her death in 1892.

Richard and Elizabeth Clarke had a family of 6 children like Francis Mager but with very little help for the business or the family. They only had one male servant and definitely no governess. It would be two daughters from the marriage to Richard who were helping Elizabeth run the Woolpack in 1871, Eliza (26) and Annie (25). There was no other staff to help her. By the 1891 census Eliza was 80 and this time assisted by her granddaughter, Annie E Turner aged 20. Eliza had died or simply given up by 1892, for the public house was then run by Anne Elizabeth Gladding until 1897.

The Ship

The Ship was built on land belonging to the feoffees of butter. This relates to a charity set up in 1575 by a Richard Wright. He bequeathed two tenements in Eastgate and 37 acres of land for the distribution of 'butter and harden cloth' to the poor of Louth. Other donations were made in later years. One of these donations was the Ship public house and an acre of land given by an unknown donor and let for around £20 in the later 19th century. By the 19th century the poor no longer had butter given to them but received money instead. The land on which the Ship stood was not owned by the Canal Commissioners. As already noted access to the Ship was via Occupation Road which in the early 19th century was in the hands of the owner of the Woolpack.

The first trade directory reference to the Ship is in 1822, when a William Cartwright was the publican. From 1828 to the early 1830s Pigot's directory names Ann Hancock as the licensee. It is a noticeable feature of both the public houses at the Riverhead that women played a significant role as the named licensee as well as in their general management. By 1835 she had been replaced by a William Jackson. In the 1841 census a John Jackson aged 40 was the licensed victualler, helped only by his wife, Susan and one female servant. The Ship was a much smaller establishment in 1841, than that run at the same time by Francis Mager at the Woolpack. Mager had a large family and a large complement of servants to help him run the inn.

By 1849 the Ship was in the hands of John Meanwell (Post Office Directory). He was to run it until 1871/1872. The 1871 census was the last one to name him as publican. By 1872 a John Skinn was named in White's Directory as the licensee. Thus the Ship experienced a long period of stability when the same family, the Meanwells, ran it for 23 years. This is comparable to the long tenancy of the Clarke/Hewson family at the Woolpack. The establishment that Meanwell ran was an expansion on that of the Jacksons in 1841. In 1851, there were 6 children from 2 months to 12 years. He also had more servants, there being an ostler in addition to a female house servant. This would suggest that the Ship was doing a trade in the stabling of horses.

Aerial view of the Riverhead in the 1950s

1. **The Ship Inn**
2. **The Ship Inn livery stabling**
3. **The Woolpack livery stabling**
4. **The Woolpack Inn**
5. **The canal head & associated warehouses**

This photograph demonstrates the extent of the stabling at the two public houses needed to keep the Riverhead trade running smoothly. The proximity of the public houses to each other is evidence of the volume of economic activity at the Riverhead at the height of its success. Also note the number of warehouses still remaining at this time. Slightly below the figure three to the left can be seen the old Riverhead tenements identified in Padley's survey of 1828, now demolished.

The Woolpack c1890

The Ship Inn, Alvingham, now Lock Farm, a private residence

The ostler had gone by the 1871 census as had the single female house servant. Instead there was an army of daughters who were all classed as assistants. John now aged 61 and Elizabeth his wife 48 ran the Ship with the help of 4 daughters aged from 28-15. Between them John and Elizabeth produced 11 children over 22 years.

By 1881 the Ship was a much smaller establishment. The census records just one woman as a publican's wife, Eliza Hewson 39, and her one year old son, Charles as present. However White's Directory 1882 named a Charles Hewson as licensee. He was presumably not present on the night of the census. Interestingly he was also described as a farmer. The close link between farming and the victualling trade that was demonstrated along the canal is also evident at this point at the Riverhead. This suggests a trade that a licensee saw as suitable to support other activity but not necessarily viable in its own right. The Ship remained similar in 1891 though under a different licensee. George Cartwright, 45, was helped by his wife Eliza, 50, and one female servant. There was also a lodger, a 20 year old dressmaker.

Both the Ship and Woolpack had become much smaller establishments by the 1890s.

The Riverhead Beerhouses

The period which saw the greatest activity for the Riverhead as an inland port was that which saw the most beer houses there. The trade directories show that there were 3 beer houses in 1849. This was the most ever maintained at the Riverhead. The beer retailers were William Clarke, William Chapman and John Towl.

The last one like other purveyors of beer along the canal corridor also had extra economic activities. Since in his case these required a period of apprenticeship, it would seem that beer retailing was an add-on opportunistic activity. John Towl was also a carpenter and wheelwright. No doubt he saw an opportunity to make extra income from selling beer. The opportunistic nature of beer retailing can be seen in John Towl's somewhat erratic career.

Although he appeared in directories at the Riverhead in 1849, John Towl was not present at the Riverhead in the 1851 census. But according to the Post Office Directory he was a beer retailer and carpenter at the Riverhead in 1855. However according to White's Directory of the next year he was then retailing beer in Eastgate. By 1861 John Towl was back at the Riverhead but he had dropped the beer retailing and just functioned as a carpenter and joiner. This could suggest some decline in trade and general activity at the port. It also shows how the sale of beer was very much a response to fluctuating economic circumstances. By 1864 Towl was not listed at all in trade directories.

John's son Allen, like other sons, chose not to seek employment in their father's line of business at the Riverhead. He moved away to Newmarket where he continued his father's trade as a wheelwright only. By 1864, he was listed as a builder at 33 Newmarket (Johnson's Directory).

Prior to 1849, the earliest reference to beer retailing comes in Pigot's 1835 Directory. This refers to both William Finn and William Chapman at the Riverhead. John Towl appears to have taken Finn's place by 1842 (White's Directory). William Chapman continued until at least 1849 when W. Clarke joined him and Towl. It was William

Clarke who remained as the second beer retailer until at least 1864 (Johnson's Directory). He is recorded in 1863 as living at 9 Thames Street (Morris & Co.). In the 1851 census he had one female servant aged13, his wife, her sister and a daughter of 14.

By the 1871 census there was only one beer retailer at the Riverhead. This was William Finney who had taken over the premises run by William Clarke at 9 Thames Street. This was known as the Lock Tavern. It only had a 6 day license as Methodist opposition in the area prevented Sunday opening here at least, although not at the Woolpack and Ship.

Finney was helped only by his wife, Sarah. His two resident children sought other means of earning an income. His son 15 was working as a lawyer's clerk, whilst his daughter Eliza 23 and unmarried was a dressmaker. In 1891, William Finney is still at 9 Thames Street aged 69. His wife was still alive. An unmarried daughter Lizzie was living with them but was not listed as having any occupation. Since her age was given as 39 it is not clear if she was the same as the Eliza 23 mentioned in 1871.

The profile of beer retailing at the Riverhead accurately matches that of the history of general economic activity there. The beer houses were most thriving from 1849 to the mid 1850s. The households maintained at the two larger licensed premises also aged and shrank over time. It was only in the period 1841- 1871 that large young families were maintained along with servants at the Ship and Woolpack. The beer houses were much more susceptible than the larger licensed premises to economic changes and can be seen as a real barometer of trading patterns.

The Raven

The Raven was the first beerhouse along the canal after leaving Louth and the Riverhead. It was situated on Eastfield Road next to the towpath. The first reference to it so far is in 1831, in the deeds of the house. However it was not described as a beer house on the deeds until later. The property described in an agreement of 4 June, 1831 was extensive. It comprised 2 cottages, 2 gardens, 4 workshops, 2 sheds and 2 outbuildings.

Despite many changes of ownership throughout the 19th and early 20th centuries it does not seem to have been much reduced by sales of parts of the property. In 1896 it is described in a deed as ' all that messuage or tenement with the yard, outbuildings and piece or parcel of garden.' There may have been some reduction by 1920 when it was sold, and described as 'all that messuage or dwelling house used as a beerhouse called the Raven Inn with the cottage adjoining.'

The size of the property at the Raven and its outbuildings is probably explained by the occupations of its first owner Joseph Atkin. He was listed in Pigot's Directory of 1835 both as a cabinet maker and joiner as well as a beer retailer. It is likely that he had the Raven built both as a home and business premises. This would explain the workshops, sheds and outbuildings. Such an arrangement was typical of pre-factory domestic industry. The beerhouse was most likely a secondary business. After Joseph Atkin, the Raven seemed to be owned by different individuals to those who ran it as tenants as a beerhouse. There was much more stability of tenant than owner particularly from the 1870s.

There were nine owners of the Raven after its only owner/publican. One of them, John Sudbury was the publican of another pub in Louth, the Three Tuns on Upgate in 1843. At least three others were brewers and would have used the Raven as a business opportunity providing an outlet for their own beer. It is possible that Sudbury was also doing that. The Birketts, brewers in the Cornmarket, owned it in 1881, Thomas Overton East of the East brewing company of Maiden Row Louth in the 1890s and Soulby Sons and Winch brewers of Alford in the early 1900s. They were presumably all using the Raven as a tied house.

The reason for the interest of another owner would be linked to his family's land holding in the area. In the late 1890s this was Sir William Earle Welby Gregory described as landowner of Denton Manor Lincolnshire in the deeds. In Padley's Survey 1828, an ancestor, Sir William Earle Welby Gregory, had been the major land owner in the neighbouring parish of Keddington. He had owned 15 out of a total of 26 blocks of land in the parish. Sir William had also owned one plot of land in Alvingham 3 miles down the canal from the Raven. There were very strong links between farmers and public house owning along the canal corridor. Sir William Earle Welby Gregory is the only known member of the gentry also to do this.

An interesting feature is that all the people who ran The Raven as a beerhouse after Joseph Atkin were described by the census as agricultural labourers. It would seem that they did not rely solely on the sale of beer for their livelihood. Furthermore, even though William Fytche was described as a beer retailer in the trade directory in 1849, in the 1851 census he was simply listed as an agricultural labourer. He was then aged 33 and had been born in Louth. He and his wife Jane had three children who were all born in the parish of Louth Park. By 1861 William Fytche was listed firstly as an agricultural labourer and then as a beerhouse keeper. His two eldest sons were not mentioned, so may have left home. The household also included John Ely 41, an agricultural labourer as a lodger. This would be another addition to the family income. By 1871 William the son had returned and was listed as a jobber. His father still had the two occupations as above. The beerhouse could not support the sons as well.

The inhabitants of the Raven had changed by 1881. It was no longer the Fytche family. Neither was the head of household described as a beerhouse keeper but as an agricultural labourer. The building itself was called the Raven Inn. The head of household then was Christopher Hewson 67. In 1891 the Raven was run by John Waller 43 and his wife Jane 41. He is described as a publican. He also had been an agricultural labourer in 1881. There is reference to him as such at Burwell in the census for that year. It seems they chose to change their form of livelihood.

Mrs. Jane Waller is referred to as a beer retailer in Kelly's Directory for 1909. She presumably was the widow of John who would have been 61 in 1909. Jane herself would be 59 and would have acquired the experience and skills to run the beerhouse. It would seem she was still there in 1920 as an abstract of that year describes the property as in the occupation of J. Waller. The Raven was typical of the canal side beer outlets, in that for most of its life the publicans needed other occupations as well as the sale of beer.

The Ship Inn Alvingham

The building that was used as the Ship Inn is adjacent to the canal and lock at Alvingham and close to the canal side wharves. It may have ended its life as an Inn in 1870. In that year it was called Lock Cottage and sold at the Masons Arms, Louth by auctioneers Mason and Son. It was referred to in the sale literature as recently occupied as an Inn and a flourishing coal business. It is thought it was built in 1770, when the navigation was completed to that point. ('Alvingham and N. Cockerington' J. Phil Davies) Alvingham was in the position of the Riverhead for a few years, but this was so short a time there was no opportunity for the business of an inland port to develop here. The Ship was a typical canal side multi-functional enterprise with beer as third string.

Robert Lucas is mentioned in1842 as a coal dealer and victualler (innkeeper) at the Ship. (Whites Directory) It is likely, however, that his main occupation was as a farmer. He is listed in 1828 as a landed proprietor at Alvingham who held considerable land there, adjoining the canal and the lock. (Padley's Survey) He was described in the 1851 census as a farmer of 150 acres. It would seem that Lucas saw the opportunity to develop businesses linked to the canal. The 1841 census chose to give his occupation as farmer leaving out his other two trades. At that time he was 45, his wife was 40, and they had 9 children at home, ranging in age from 20 years to one.

It is likely that Lucas brewed his own beer, possibly using barley he had grown himself. Malt was easily available from Louth. There was a maltkiln at the Riverhead where the canal reached the town. In 1851 the census lists all of his occupations, farmer, coal merchant and publican. Two of his older sons were employed on the farm, whilst 5 of his daughters were listed as servants. Some of these daughters maybe helped in the beerhouse business.

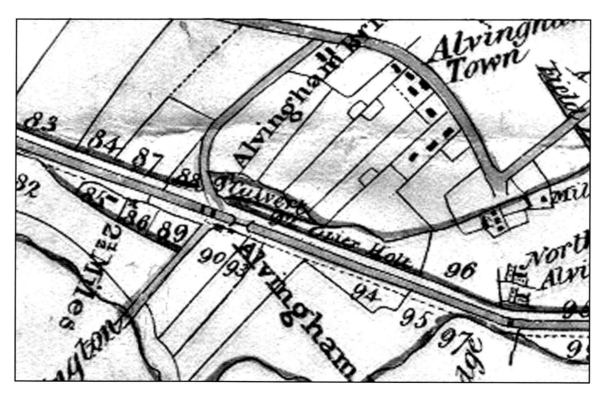

Plots 86.87. 90 & 94 adjacent to the canal, were owned by Robert Lucas and made possible his various economic activities. Plot 90 is where the Ship Inn is situated.

The Lucas family continued to be mainly involved with farming even after the sale of the public house. Two sons remained farming in the area. George, 50, in 1881 was farming 50 acres at Yarborough, which may have been part of the150 acres that his father had farmed. Albert Lucas was opposite the Ship Inn in 1881, when he was described as a farmer of 32 acres at 2, Canal Bank. This was one of a pair of cottages, no longer standing, adjacent to the lock. Thus the main economic string of Lucas family continued. It is possible that they no longer saw beer retailing, as a viable activity.

The Ship Inn Fire Beacon

Padley's Survey of 1828, describes in detail a public house, garden, coalyard and 'a small brewhouse.' It was situated near the canal at Fire Beacon Bridge. The major lessee of the canal, George Chaplin, sublet the property in 1828 to William Carter and his father Kidd Carter. It may well have had a beer house built into its original function. However, like the Ship Inn at Alvingham it had multiple functions. Kidd Carter was a farmer owning a plot of land in Grainthorpe, and another one at Marshchapel. The property included farm buildings as well. Robert Smart is mentioned as coal and corn merchant and farmer, though not as a publican in 1842, (Whites Directory). In the 1841 census the household of Robert Smart listed as a farmer, contained himself, his wife, 3 children under 4 years, 2 men servants and one Harriet Smart, aged 15 who is listed as publican. She is not listed with the 3 children and since there is such an age difference between her and them it is possible she was Robert Smart's sister used to run the beerhouse side of the family business.

The position next to the canal and bridge seems to have given rise to opportunities for linked businesses such as the sale of beer, dealings in coal and corn in addition to farming. A major road crossed the canal here, linking it and the marsh villages, of Fulstow, Grainthorpe, the Covenhams, and Marshchapel. Warehouses grew up at this point where coal, fruit and vegetables were brought in, and grain and wool was shipped out from the marsh villages and farms. Heavy goods also came in such as timber, bricks, pantiles and slates. Given the need to co-ordinate with the tides, water transport still remained quicker to Hull, than the combined rail and water route. Goods were slowed down by transfer from rail to ship at New Holland in order to cross the Humber.

John Dalton ran a grouping of businesses at the Ship in the 1850s and 1860s. White's Directory describes him as coal and corn merchant and victualler, whilst in 1861 he is described as coal and corn merchant and maltster. It is likely he was producing his own malt for brewing his beer. During the 1870s George Kirk is mentioned in Directories as a victualler at the Ship Inn. This was the same George Kirk who had been farmer and publican at the Crown and Anchor from around 1861-1868. He may have moved straight from one to the other.

The census of 1881 referred to George Kirk as a farmer of 4 acres and a licensed victualler at Fire Beacon. He was then a widower aged 63, but was assisted by his widowed daughter Elizabeth Anne, aged 31 as housekeeper. Thus George gained help around the house and possibly also in the preparation and sale of beer. He had no other servants. Elizabeth gained a home and living for herself and her 3 young daughters.

The Inns At Tetney Lock, The Crown and Anchor Public House

This inn was in existence around the time of the opening of the canal and possibly before. The community at Tetney Lock around this time was small. There were few buildings. There was possibly little more than the toll keeper's cottage, who often doubled as the lock keeper (as in the 1871 census), and the Crown and Anchor until later in the 19th century.

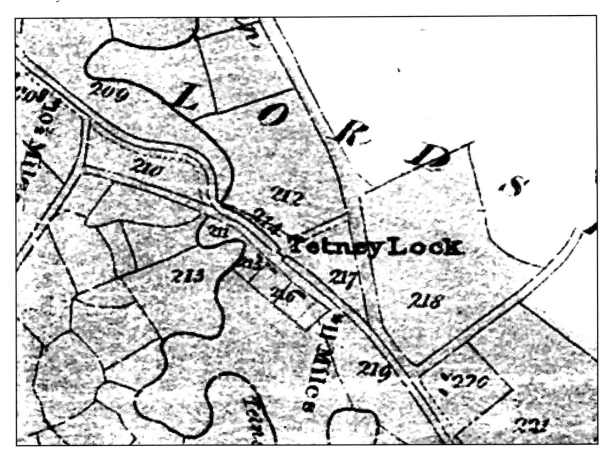

The Crown and Anchor was run by the Maughan family from at least 1792 until 1856. Padley's Survey 1828 shows plot 216 as in the ownership of Samuel Maughan and comprising two small enclosures. One had a single large building and the other two smaller buildings. One of these must have been the Crown and Anchor. The plot is opposite Tetney Lock, which is where the inn is situated. The extent of the Maughan's landholding was identified by Padley as also including plots 210, 219, 220 & 222.

The Lindsey Alehouse licensing documents refer to a Joseph Maughan of Tetney as the licensee and a William Pearson of 'Castor 'as the other applicant on the 12th September 1792. It is possible to get a fuller understanding of Joseph Maughan's social position from a collection of documents relating to the family in the Lincolnshire Archives.

Joseph was an Officer in the Excise at West Stockwith around 1770. He married Mary Martha, the youngest daughter of Joseph and Ann Radley. Her parents gave lands to the couple that they had held at Tetney on the 6th December, 1776. These comprised 15 acres of arable land, a fourth part of two closes, Greenholme and Sowgrift Moor, a cottage and 2 acres of meadow on the Ings. Joseph Maughan continued as an Officer in the Excise, now based at Tetney. However he was henceforth referred to in documents as a yeoman of Tetney. As well as being an educated civil servant he was becoming a substantial landowner. He added to the holdings arising from his marriage with the purchase of the lands of a Mr. Ludlam of Tetney Lock who had become bankrupt.

The position of licensed victualler that he took on in 1792 was a further opportunity to expand his extensive enterprises. He is referred to in the family documents as a victualler in 1794 in a property of one acre two roods known as Lockpit Closes. We can assume that this is the current position of the Crown and Anchor as it was and is directly opposite the lock. The closes are most likely the two small enclosures seen on Padley 1828. In his will Joseph nominated Edward Gray of Louth as a trustee. An Edward Gray was the father of Stephen Gray, the merchant and owner of the Woolpack at the Riverhead. This is likely evidence of contacts sharing an interest in business at both ends of the canal.

It would seem to be Joseph's son, Samuel Maughan, who was publican of the Crown and Anchor in the 1841 census. Samuel is documented as the son of Joseph and Mary Maughan and as being christened 9th July 1779. There is some discrepancy around Samuel's age as if he was born 1779, he should have been 62 not 60 in 1841. However there were broad bands for assigning ages to people born before the compulsory civil registration of births, marriages and deaths from 1839. Samuel fits into this structure.

Samuel Maughan is described as a farmer of 37 acres in the 1851 census. This is the earliest census to give such detail. He was presumably the owner of a similar amount of land in 1841. In Padley's Survey of the canal 1828, Samuel is listed as owning five plots of land in Tetney (210, 216, 219, 220 and 222). These were adjacent to holdings by George Chaplin and Sir Montague Cholmeley. The Maughans were landowners of some significance in Tetney. That they chose to run the Crown and Anchor would suggest that they saw an inn at this location as a good commercial venture.

The Maughan household of 21 people in 1841 was very numerous. It comprised Samuel Maughan, his wife Elizabeth and 9 children aged between 1-18 years. In addition there were 3 people of independent means living at the inn. They were Samuel's brother John Thomas aged 50, Sarah Chatterton, 60 and Ann Chatterton, 20, presumably her daughter. There were also 5 male servants. Two further female servants completed the 1841 household. They could have been either for the house or the farm.

In 1851 there were 7 children. The eldest son John remained, earning a living as a coal merchant. However, the 3 siblings beneath him, Elizabeth, Henry and George had left home. There had been the addition of another daughter, Mary Martha, 6, in the intervening ten years. Samuel and Elizabeth had been producing children until he was around 65 and she was around 40. The 1851 census described him as a victualler, wharfinger and farmer.

The family papers show that land holding and farming were historically the Maughan family's main economic activity. Running the inn and the coal business at the wharf was added later as secondary, opportunistic enterprises exploiting their position as land owners adjacent to the Lock and wharf. It is likely, that like many other publicans at the time Samuel brewed his own beer. He was described as a maltster in White's directory 1856. The production of malt was a natural outcome of his farming using barley he had grown. He could have used this to brew beer on his own premises

Two views of the Crown & Anchor, Tetney Lock. Above late 19th century, below as it is today. Note the warehouse on the left has been converted into a private residence.

Firebeacon Bridge today showing the old warehouse complex. The Ship Inn faced it across the canal.

Austin Fen Warehouse.

The total household in 1851 comprised 18 residents, only 3 less than in 1841. The farm and inn were still an economically thriving concern. Brother John Thomas now identified as a retired master mariner still lived there as did Sarah Chatterton described as an annuitant, and born in Finningley in Yorkshire.

The 1851 census gives a much clearer picture of the reasons for employing the 6 servants. Along with the eldest son John as a coal merchant there were 3 men employed as farm servants and coal porters. A young boy of 14 was employed just as a farm servant, and a female as a dairy maid. One other woman functioned as a house servant. Isaac Chapman, agricultural labourer was a visitor. This profile of the servants at the Crown and Anchor shows it functioned as an enterprise and employment hub that integrated farming, hospitality and coal trading. The last two were integrally linked to the canal. Samuel's trade as a wharfinger would seem to have been mainly in coal.

The Maughan link with the Crown and Anchor carried on after Samuel. According to White's Directory, Samuel ten years the elder was succeeded as publican by his brother, the retired master mariner in 1856. John Thomas would have been aged around 68 by this time. He did not remain many years for by the census of 1861 the innkeeper was George Kirk. John Thomas Maughan, brother of Samuel left Tetney Lock went to live in Grimsby, for it was here at The Abbey that he drew up his will in 1863. A diary kept by Samuel Maughan's eldest son John, 1888-1890 shows that he was still a landholder of some standing in Tetney Lock. He farmed 25 acres of pasture and 6 acres of meadow.

George Kirk was a farmer but on a smaller scale than the Maughans. The Maughan land holding had been separated from the inn. There is a possibility that the Maughans may still have owned the Crown and Anchor but no longer ran it as licensees. George Kirk had only half their land holding, at 18 acres. He did employ 3 men but they were not indoor servants. The family comprised George, his wife and 6 children between 1 and 13. They only had one living in servant, a female aged 17. George was not listed as a wharfinger, and there is no mention of the coal trade. By the 1870s George Kirk had moved down the canal to a very similar business, the Ship at Fire Beacon. Here he was also a publican and farmer. In addition there were wharves and warehouses.

Charles Mumby had taken over as publican by 1868 (Kelly's Directory). He too ran the inn as a secondary enterprise alongside farming. White's directory 1872 also showed that Mumby continued the business in coal dealing with which the Maughans had been involved. Trade based on proximity to the wharves was still a factor. The 1871 census does not give the acreage held by Mumby. The family enterprise would seem to be on a much smaller scale than that of the Maughans. The household was smaller, Charles being assisted by one son, also Charles aged 22, and his daughter Mary aged 19. She is classed as an assistant. Maybe she helped in the inn, alongside the only servant, a female aged 16.

The link between running the inn and farming was finally broken by 1881, when the census refers to William Stones as the innkeeper. He is not given as having any other occupation. The household was very small and suggests that trade was limited. William was 50 and assisted only by his wife aged 46 and a female domestic servant, 15. Ten years later, in 1891, William Stones had left the Crown and Anchor and was simply classed as an agricultural cottager at Tetney Lock with his wife Harriet as the total household. The family was very different to previous publicans. There was a vast social gap between the Stones and established and wealthy landowners such as the Maughans, and to a lesser extent, George Kirk.

The last family to run the Crown and Anchor whilst the canal was still functioning was the Drewrys. They had the inn until almost the end of the canal in 1922. Alfred Drewry had a completely different background to previous publicans. Like others it was not necessarily his main occupation. He was listed as living in Albion Street Grimsby in the 1881 census and working as an engine fitter.

Alfred's background was urban and industrial unlike most of the other publicans who were linked to the rural and agricultural sphere. He was running the Crown and Anchor by 1891. But he had carried on as a craftsman and whitesmith running a small business from the inn. His eldest son was not identified by the census as assisting him in the running of the inn. Instead he was functioning as a whitesmith helping his father in his other trade. It was his wife, Hannah who was listed as publican. There was an elder daughter of 21 and four other children between 8 –16. There were no servants at all. Albert Drewry was the licensee at the Crown and Anchor until at least 1919. Kelly's directory lists William Atkinson as licensee by 1922. Drewry would have been around 75 when he ceased to be the publican and virtually remained until the canal itself ceased functioning in 1924.

The history of the publicans at the Crown and Anchor show an enterprise that became increasingly unattractive as an extra economic activity to local farmers. Presumably this was because there was some decline in trade both for the inn and in goods on the wharf. There was a world of difference between the Maughans, substantial landowners, and an artisan family like the Drewrys. Where the Maughan children of 1841-1851 can be tracked down they did well. One, Samuel became a G.P., and Cecilia married the vicar of Tetney. They enjoyed a secure professional middle class status.

The Crown and Anchor, unlike other public houses along the canal remains to this day. It still serves the locals and those visiting Tetney Lock.

The Sloop Inn

The Sloop arose as much from the needs of the small but growing community at Tetney Lock, as from the trade generated by the canal. Samuel Maughan was the only entry for Tetney Lock in the 1849 Post Office Directory of 1849. By the latter part of the 19th century there were around ten entries for the hamlet. This is an interesting comparison to the Riverhead in Louth where there was stagnation from the 1850s to 1880s and some decline in population by the 1890s.

It was presumably this growth at Tetney Lock that Stephen Hartley was responding to when he set up his shop there around 1861 (Post Office Directory). There was no shop mentioned in White's 1856 Directory. Hartley's shop had grown to include a beer retail outlet by the 1871 census. Hartley was referred to there as both shopkeeper and publican. It must have been a small affair, as he was only assisted by his wife Elizabeth, and a niece of 17. Hartley and his wife were in their 50s. There seems to have been some rapid changes of ownership around 1880. The 1881 census named a George Burton as running the beer house at Tetney Lock but in White's Directory of 1882 this had changed to Joseph Cook.

Mr. Hundleby ran the beer house and shop at Tetney Lock from at least the 1891 census until 1937. In 1891 he is referred to as a licensed victualler. He is also described as a farmer. If so he was similar to Robert Lucas and other farmers and publicans along the canal. The business gained a grander name and designation by 1901 when it was referred to as the Sloop Inn under Hundleby's management in the census of that year. There was only Henry, 45 and his wife Minnie, 30, to run both inn and grocery shop. There was however no mention of Henry as a farmer in 1901. He had also been designated a carrier in Kelly's Directory of 1896. Thus, the premises were like the other canal side ventures, with beer retailing as a part of a multi-functional business. The Sloop no longer exists although the premises it inhabited still remain.

THE LOUTH STEAM NAVIGATION COMPANY (1886)

One of the major problems the vessels faced was the wind. If it was coming out of the east, 'the winds in Tetney 'ole', is still a saying today although it means the wind is cold. In the days of sail it simply meant the ships could not navigate out of Tetney Haven into the Humber. Some craft were stuck there for a week or more. We have seen that Mr Chaplin purchased a steam vessel to tow the ships out of the Haven into the Humber mouth in an attempt to solve this problem.

One group of Louth gentlemen came up with a solution to overcome this problem. They decided to form a company and purchase a steam ship. The Louth Steam Navigation Company was formed at a meeting held on the 28th June 1886, and duly registered under the Companies Acts, 1862 to 1880 on the 18th October 1886. It was a company limited by shares. At the time of formation the company consisted of the following Directors:

James Fowler, Grove House, Louth, Architect

Jonathan Hurst, 176 Eastgate, Louth, Chemist

Richard J Nell, James Street, Louth, Merchant

John W Barton, Aswell Lane, Louth, Corn Merchant

Bryan Hall, George Street, Louth, Corn Miller

Daniel D Richardson, Wellington Hotel, Wellington Street, Louth, Hotel Keeper

Saville Smith, Bridge Street, Louth, Wholesale Grocer

The capital of the company was to be £2000, in one hundred shares of £20 each; £15 was to be paid up at the time of the company's formation. The Directors were to hold one share each. However, records show that by the 2nd November of that year Smith held 5 shares. Barton, Hall, Nell and Hurst each held 3 shares. Whilst Fowler and Richardson held 1 share each. The total value of the Directors 19 shares came to £380.

A list of subscribers published on 2nd November 1886 indicates there were 41 shareholders having 82 shares between them worth £1640. The principal shareholder was Sheardown and Barter who held 10 shares. Furley and Company of Hull (the Company's Agents) held 7 shares and Arther Wood, of Hull, held a further 5 shares. The Company's Bankers were Messrs. Garfitt, Claypon and Co. of 24 Mercer Row, Louth.

The Company's first annual report was issued on 14th February 1888, covering the period from foundation to 31st December 1887. The main purpose of the Company, the report states, was to establish regular and competitive communication between Louth and Hull. Trading with Hull was subject to the tide and weather. Barges were often held up at Tetney Lock because of the lack of wind or the wind blowing in the wrong direction preventing the craft from leaving the Haven.

As a first step the Directors had a steamship built, the ss Luda, by the Sunderland Steamship Building Company at a cost of £1250. Her first trip to Louth was on the 8th

January 1887. The Directors discovered that the carrying capacity of the Luda was insufficient for their needs and that the ship was, therefore, not suited to Canal traffic. It seems amazing that the Directors did not realise they required a craft that could carry at least 50 tons before they went ahead and bought the Luda!

It was decided to dispose of the ship as quickly as possible if a good offer could be found. Fortunately for the investors the Admiralty wanted such a vessel, and she was disposed of on favourable terms, the only condition being immediate delivery, which the company was able to meet. The sale price was £1650 giving the Company a profit of some £200 after insurance and commission had been deducted.

The sale of the ss Luda left the Directors with a problem. They had no ship with which to carry on trading with Hull. They had to come up with a solution rather quickly to avoid considerable loss of income. They engaged Sloops to cover this period. However, Sloops were, as we know, subject to the tide and favourable winds with which to sail. Often this did not meet the weekly commitment of trips to Hull. A small Steam Tug, the Cicada, was used to solve the problem. It was able to negotiate the Humber and the Navigation so keeping up the weekly visits. There was a price to pay for this in the charges of both tug and sloop.

The cost of chartering the Sloops and the Cicada was £505. So the profit made on the sale of the first Luda was swallowed up in the additional expense of chartering.

The Managing Director of the Company, Mr. Richard J Nell being mindful of the loss of profitable trade and expense of chartering had purchased, at his own expense, a Steam Barge, the Lindsey. Nell considered the barge would give the Company good service. The Directors, having inspected the vessel, decided to reimburse Mr. Nell at the cost price of £580. In the Company's first annual report it stated that the Lindsey had done good service since its purchase.

A steam barge was a converted Sloop or Keel. Part of the rear cabin had been altered to accommodate a steam engine to power the vessel. However, this would have cut its carrying capacity considerably as a steam engine took up a great deal of space.

In the meantime the Directors set about replacing the Luda with a new vessel. They sought tenders for another Steam Ship better suited to the nature of canal traffic. They obtained plans from two companies.

After due consideration, the order was given to Mr. E Wales of Hull. The new ship was once again to be named the Luda. The vessel was handed to the Company on the 30th August 1887. The Directors were satisfied with their new acquisition as it could carry almost 30 tons more than the old Luda.

The construction of the new vessel, which cost £1073-3s-7d, had not been long in construction and one wonders if the workmanship was all that could be desired as three years later repairs to the vessel amounted to £37-9s-10d. That is around £1500 in today's terms.

The Company was facing a further problem at this time. The wharf side, for unloading, was too low for the Luda. The Directors had been in negotiation with the Canal

Commissioners but to no avail. It was decided to build an Iron Shed with raised platform in order to provide the rapid and economical discharge of their boats, yet more expense. A photograph taken around the turn of the nineteenth century clearly shows the shed and platform sited on the Thames Street side of the Riverhead Basin, approximately half way along the wharf side.

At the end of the first year of trading the Directors expressed themselves satisfied with the volume of goods transported to and from Hull despite the problems they had experienced with the first Luda. The total tonnage carried to 31st December 1887 was 6330 tons. However, the Directors had failed to solve the problem of carrying the traffic at a profit to the shareholders. There was considerable dissatisfaction amongst the investors over the management of the Company by the Directors.

Their problem was in fixing the rates at a level sufficiently low to secure the trade, and sufficiently high to be profitable. The first years trading resulted in a loss on their capital. The Directors expressed themselves disappointed with the results and hoped the shareholders would attend the annual meeting on 23rd February when these and other matters would be discussed. There was little need to state this to the Shareholders.

By that time Daniel Richardson and Jonathan Hurst had left the Board of Directors to be replaced by Issac J Colbridge and John C Barker. The Managing Director and Company Secretary at this time was Richard Nell. The registered office was 20 Corn Market, Louth and their bankers were Garfit, Claypon, and Co., of Louth. The chairman of the Company was Saville Smith.

The Annual Meeting was not a great success for the Directors as the shareholders were less than happy with the Companies losses. They demanded that something should be done. A joint committee consisting of the Directors and five Shareholders was appointed to investigate the affairs of the Company, and to consider the question of future management.

By the time the Company presented its second annual report the Directors had shrunk to five; Saville Smith remained Chairman along with John Barton, Bryan Hall, Isaac Colbridge and James Fowler as the remaining Directors. However, as a result of the joint committee Mr. John Charles Barker, of Hull, had been appointed as Honorary Manager of the Company.

The Directors had found it necessary to call in the final £5 of the £20 shares, so the Company was now had its maximum capital of £2000, around £80 000 in today's money.

During 1888 the Directors were able to report that under the management of Mr. Barker great improvements had been made. This had resulted in a small balance in Company finances for the final 3 quarters of the year (April to December). They were able to state that the Companies property had been maintained in a thorough state of efficiency with various improvements being made to both the Luda and the Lindsey.

However, a glance at the Companies balance sheet for the year shows a decrease in the value of the Lindsey of some £373. Its original value in 1887 when purchased was £578 and by February 1889 its value was down to £205. The Luda, on the other hand, had increased in value by 30%, going from £1085 to £1410.

Having made a small profit in the last 3 quarters of 1888 the Directors had to report a drop in the gross tonnage carried by its steamships in the year, 5062 tons had been transported, a drop on the previous year of 1268 tons.

The Directors put this drop down to competition from other water transport, Sloops, Keels and Billyboys etc. and from a poor harvest that year. But it was mostly as a result of competition from the Railway Company who had reduced their rates to encourage more business. However, they stated that there had not been a diminution on the general goods traffic.

Having stated all this they still had not solved the problem of securing a reduction in the Canal dues to which they felt the Company entitled. They hoped the Navigation Commissioners would look upon their request for a reduction favourably.

It has to be said that the Commissioners themselves were facing their own problems over profitability of the Canal at that time so the Steam Navigation Company stood little chance of success in their bid to have the rates reduced.

There would no doubt have been more muttering and murmuring amongst the Shareholders regarding their investment, despite the final 3 quarters of 1888 showing a small profit. Although some of them may have been optimistic for the forth coming year.

Trading continued during 1889 but had once again fallen. It was down by 927 tons to 4135 tons. In the Directors annual report they expressed themselves satisfied with the volume of traffic for the year. This may not have been the shareholders view however. In the past three years gross tonnage had fallen by 35% from 6330 to 4135 tons. This fall matches the fortunes of the Canal at the time.

The profit on the trade carried for that year was £1437-8-3. With its outgoings of £1527-12-4 it had to carry a trading loss of £90-4-1. Not a happy situation for the shareholders when they had seen a small profit the year before.

The Directors placed the blame for the years fall in profits on the Canal having been closed for a considerable period. The Canal had long suffered from silting up and sections were regularly stopped to allow for dredging and could take as long as six weeks to complete.

The Directors reported that they were still unable to carry traffic at a profit to the shareholders and 1889 had seen a loss of, £99-4-1. In their defence the Directors also blamed part of the loss on the Luda having been docked and thoroughly overhauled at considerable cost. In fact the Company records show £37-9-10 was spent on those repairs. This would represent around £1700 in to day's money. A considerable amount considering the Luda was less than three years old!

They reported that the Canal's Commissioners had made some concessions regarding the reduction in Canal rates but that they were unlikely to come into operation before the end of 1890.

The report only mentions the Luda and not the Lindsey. A glance at the accounts for the year 1889 shows there was a loss on the Lindsey of £34-8-3. However, it does not give us any clues as to the fate of the Lindsey.

As has been stated, the Canal's Commissioners were having their own problems at the time. Competition from the railway was fierce. In an attempt to overcome this, the Commissioners had reduced the rates to the lowest level they could. However, this still did not prevent the inevitable shift of traffic to the railways.

The canal traffic was subject to the vagaries of the weather and the frequent stopping of the canal for repair.

They had set up a committee to consider this vexed issue in 1893. The report had eight observations to make. The final one was quite illuminating as far as steam traffic on the canal was concerned.
It stated:
> "We feel it most important to carry on the steamer traffic, as it is a source of income which may some day develop."

No doubt this was added as a gentle prod to the barge owners to have their vessels converted to steam power and so ensure a regular service independent of the weather.

This may well have been the case with the sloop Reliance, owned by Mr. A Mc. G. Nell, for a paper written by Mr. J W White in a speech to the Louth Naturalists, Antiquarian and Literacy Society lists, among arrivals and departures at the Riverhead, the ss Reliance.

During 1893 there had been a period of eight weeks of storms when barges were unable to move. This lost the Commissioners an estimated £300 in income, not an inconsiderable sum in those days. The situation towards the middle 1890's was becoming quite desperate for them.

Whites Directory for 1892/3 informs us that 'a small steamer runs regularly between Louth and Hull'. By 1896 Kelly's Directory states 'The Louth Steam Navigation Company' was still trading on a weekly basis between Louth and Hull. By now it had a new Manager, Mr. Joseph Harvey, who lived at 91 James Street in Louth.

THE BLOT BEGINS TO BITE

The Great Northern Railway Company continued to run the navigation for the remainder of its 29 years lease. The Navigation was still used and, as old photographs testify, much trade passed up and down the canal. However, it was a losing battle. As the railways improved, more and more businesses transferred to this quicker means of transportation. In March of 1876, when the lease was about to end, the general manager of the G.N.R., Henry Oakley, sent the following account to the Board of Directors.

	£	s	d
Receipts Year 1875	1,807	5	7
Expenses	1,104	7	6

Profit on Working	702	18	1
Interest on Mortgages	1,545	12	0

Net Loss	842	13	11

Oakley then made the following recommendations:

> ..."If this canal passes into the hands of private owners it will, of course, become a competitor with us for the Louth traffic and the tolls which we have purposely kept up to the highest legal rate will no doubt be lowered and the trade on the canal encouraged. By the Act constituting the canal the tolls are to be let by auction every year and the Louth Commissioners are, at present, considering what course they should take.....Though we may be exposed to some little loss by the competition of the canal I think, on the whole, we had better abstain from interference and if at the end of a year or two we find that, for any reason, it is desirable to obtain re-possession of the canal, we should no doubt be able to compete for it at the annual auction and give better terms than any outside parties would be able to afford, but for the present, it appears to me desirable not to interfere unless application be, in the first instance, made to us...."

The G.N.R. board minuted the following on the 17th March 1876: "Recommendation approved."

On the 5th July 1876 the Canal Commissioners wrote to the G.N.R. to inform them there would be a meeting on the 15th July, for accepting tenders, and enquiring whether the G.N.R. would apply. Oakley again reported to the board in a way which showed he had not changed his mind regarding the issue.

As a result of Oakley's second report to the board they decided to make no offer for the tolls. The auction for the tolls was organised for the 8th June 1876, unfortunately there were no bidders, so the Commissioners took the collection, for the time being, into their own hands.

Riverhead c.1880. The number of boats illustrates the considerable amount of trade that was still carried out as late as thirty-two years after the arrival of the railway.

The Riverhead c.1910. The lack of boats illustrates the decline in trade at this time.

Two illustrations showing the damage caused by the Louth Flood of 1920 at Riverhead. This disaster was the final blow which led to the formal closure of the canal in 1924.

THE END IS NIGH

After three months, during which time £388 had been collected, a lessee was found and the tolls were let for the remainder of the year for the sum of £566 making a total of £954 for the year. For 1878 and 1879 the lease was for £755, for 1880, £864, and for 1881, £900. In 1882 the leaseholder defaulted after paying only £225 and the collection reverted to the Commissioners who collected another £774, a total of £999 for the year. During this year the tolls were reduced but the returns continued to be satisfactory until after the turn of the century.

The main traffic on the canal had always been in the export of corn and wool, and the import of coal. However, the competition from the railway made the Commissioners rethink their strategy and look for new sources of traffic. On the 20th June, 1887, they reported they were in negotiation with the Aire and Calder Navigation, on grain rates. The negotiations were successful and the traffic, in wheat, increased to the Leeds and Wakefield area.

It was at this time that the third Act of Parliament was granted. It set out new toll rates in an attempt to compete with the railways. The items listed give a picture of those commodities still being traded on the Navigation.

TABLE OF TOLLS

From and After the 24th June, 1887

		s	d
1	For every Ton of Sugar, Molasses, Currants, Raisins & Figs	1	8
2	For every Ton of Slate, Timber, Deals & Freestone	1	8
3	For every Ton of Coals	1	0
4	For every Forty Bushels of Cinders, Coke or Culm	1	0
5	For every Eighty Tods of Wool, of 28 lbs to each Tod	2	0
6	For every One Thousand of Stock Bricks, Paving Bricks, Floor bricks, or Pantiles	2	0
7	For every One Thousand Common Bricks	1	0
8	For every Quarter of Rye Grass Seed and Hay Seed	0	2
9	For every Twelve Bunches of plaster Laths	0	4
10	For every Quarter of Wheat, Beans, Peas, Lentils, Barley, Malt, Oats, Rape Seed or Linseed	0	4
11	For every Ton of Cotton Seed, Bones, Bone Ash, Guano, Vitriol, Super Phosphates and other Artificial Manures	1	6
12	For every Ton of Cotton Oil, Linseed Oil, Rape Oil and Gas Tar manufactured in Louth	1	4
13	For every Ton or Chaldron of Lime	1	6
14	For every Ton of Farm Manure, Night Soil, Granite, Gravel, Slag, and other Road Material	0	9
15	For every Ton of all other Goods, Wares, and merchandise	1	8

The vast majority of the goods listed in the tolls above were imports and only a small minority were exports. For example wheat and wool remained an export along with cotton, linseed and rape oil. Night soil was taken out to sea and dumped by the bucket and chuck-it method.

For a time the new tolls appeared to have maintained its revenue. However, the inevitable was bound to happen and the tolls began their rapid decline two years later as more and more traffic moved to the railway. The imbalance of imports over exports noted in 1828 clearly continued.

For instance in 1900, 15,922 tons of goods were imported in Louth whilst only 2276 tons were exported. This continued until 1916 when the traffic had virtually ceased. The following table shows the receipts for selected years and emphasises the rapid decline in the early twentieth century:

Year	£	Year	£	Year	£
1887	1,417	1902	874	1912	453
1898	1,026	1903	659	1913	410
1900	932	1904	553	1914	375
1901	939	1911	407	1915	160
				1916	66

It was at this point that the First World War intervened. The restriction of shipping in the Humber and the absence of other inland routes undoubtedly hastened the end of regular traffic and the closure of the canal.

It had been recognised that the canal was in trouble well before this time for, in 1895, the rector of North Coates wrote this letter to the Commissioners, in the hope of raising extra income to aid the canal:

> Dear Sir,
> You are perhaps not aware what a popular place, for excursionists, Tetney Lock is becoming. I think your Canal Company should be up and doing. A pretty little steamboat for pleasure trips to Louth and back would be, I think, a decided success. A few nice boats also, for rowing parties, would form a profitable investment, and why not let an acre or two of land and make Tetney Lock Gardens, which would make the mouths, of Sheffield people, water. Houses, also, are much wanted in which comfortable apartments could be had. There is a general concurrence of feeling that there is nothing nicer than a stroll along the canal to Thoresby Bridge and along the sea bank to the Haven. Please regard this as merely a private communication and believe me.
>
> Yours very truly
> T. R. Matthews.

The Commissioners totally ignored the letter, which is a great pity, as those facilities may still have existed to this day.

On the 29th May 1920 the Louth flood occurred, with considerable loss of life and property. Barges were lifted clear of the basin and all manner of flotsam and jetsam was washed down into the Riverhead area, causing considerable damage. This was the last straw, and an application was made, in that same year, to the Ministry Of Transport asking for an order to relieve the Commissioners from all liability to maintain the canal. The order was granted on the 16th June 1924 and the navigation was abandoned.

The Town Council had one last attempt to change the mind of the Commissioners, at a council meeting on 8th April, when one councillor made a strong plea for its retention. The motion was lost as only the proposer and seconder voted for it. They did agree, however, to take over and reconstruct the bridges. This was in agreement with the Rural District Council, although £1500 had been contributed by the Commissioners from the sale of property.

On the 5th September the annual general meeting took place. Shortly afterwards the sale of property took place. Houses were sold for £60 and £70 each. The total proceeds of the sale, which included most of the property round the Riverhead at Louth, and a smallholding at Fulstow, reached £6240. In 1927 the residue of funds was distributed to the mortgagees at the rate of just under 11.5% of the original mortgage.

Today the swing and fixed bridges have long since disappeared to be replaced by modern road bridges. The lock gates have either rotted or been removed. Keddington Church Lock was dismantled because of its poor state. Its walls replaced by wire baskets filled with the original bricks. Out Fen and Salter Fen Locks have had parts of their walls removed. This is because of scouring at their up-stream end where the waters of the Lud fall over the sills and undermine the clay base of the lock pit.

The Louth Navigation Trust has dedicated itself to the preservation of what is left of the canal and its buildings. They have been successful in having several of the Riverhead buildings "listed". The Woolpack and the two warehouses at the 'Head' of the canal were listed in the early 1990's. This was followed by Baines watermill. They have been responsible for renewing part of the tow path just after Top Lock. They have carried out repairs to Ticklepenny Lock helping preserve it for future generations. They also regularly cut the tow path so it can be used as a Public Right of Way down to Tetney for those who wish to walk all or part of the route.

They have replaced the floor of the lock pit, which was badly undercut at the upper sill, with concrete and have done a certain amount of repointing the brickwork. Their hope, of course, is that one day the canal will be restored to its former glory and boats will once again be able to travel from Tetney to Louth.

As a start they have linked up with Groundwork Lincs to restore the old warehouse to the left of the Riverhead. The project began in 1998 and the warehouse was opened in April 1999.

For the present the waters continue to flow out of Louth and down to Alvingham and so across the open marshes to Tetney and the Humber. Keels and Sloops no longer make that journey, driven by the seamarsh winds or towed by a horse. The waters are left to flow by themselves to the sound of the marsh birds and the occasional walker, a constant reminder of Louth's glorious past. But things may yet change. The Feasibility Study of 2005 can be seen as the replacement for Grundy's plans and we are hoping to start again.

Sources

The First Minute Book of the Louth Navigation Commissioners 1760 – 1828.
The Second Minute Book, which commenced in 1882.
Letters and papers relating to the Tolls. LAO
Navigation Scheme for Tetney Haven to Louth. J. Grundy/J Smeaton
Lincoln, Rutland and Stamford Mercury.
Whites Directories 1842, 1856, and 1872.
Pigot & Co Directories 1822, 1835 and 1841.
Kelly's Directories, 1868, 1900 and 1913, 1922.
A History of Lincolnshire – A Rogers
Louth Canal – Description of the Locks, Bridges &c. J S Padley – 1828.
Census Returns – 1841, 1851, 1861, 1871, 1881, 1891 and 1901.
Universal British Directory - 1791
A History of Grimsby – E. Gillett.
The Three Acts of Parliament for the Navigation – 1763, 1828 and 1886
Lincolnshire Town and Industry 1770 - 1914. Neil R Wright
The Book of Louth. David Robinson
Eastern Part of Louth. A Paper by J. W. White
Eastern End of the Town – Story of the Navigation. A Paper by J. W. White
Papers Relating to the Louth Steam Navigation Company. SMS
Papers and Letters Relating to the Navigation. LNT Archive
The Engineering Works of John Grundy. A. W. Skempton
John Grundy of Spalding – Engineer 1719 – 1783. Neil R Wright
Louth Navigation – Engineering Aspects. D. Carnell and H. S. Waddington
Humber Keels and Keel Men. Fred Schofield
Humber Keel and Sloop Preservation Society Achieve. Brian Peeps
A History of Louth. J. E. Swaby
Louth Industrial Trail. Louth Teachers Centre
1828 OS Map of Louth and District
1805 Enclosure map
The Nell Family resources supplied by Patricia Williams of New Zealand (granddaughter of R J Nell)
Post Offices Directories 1849, 1861.
Records of Ship Repairs (1892 to 1914) at Wray and Smith Shipyards. LNT Archive.
The Maughan Family Papers, Lincs Archive.
Photographs are from the authors own collection unless otherwise stated.